VERB YOUR ENTHUSIASM

Also by Sarah L. Kaufman

The Art of Grace

VERB Your Enthusiasm

How to Master
the Art of the Verb
and
Transform Your Writing

SARAH L. KAUFMAN

PENGUIN PRESS NEW YORK 2026

PENGUIN PRESS
An imprint of Penguin Random House LLC
1745 Broadway, New York, NY 10019
penguinrandomhouse.com

Book design by Daniel Lagin

LIBRARY OF CONGRESS CATALOGING-IN-PUBLICATION DATA
Names: Kaufman, Sarah L., author
Title: Verb your enthusiasm: how to master the art of the verb
and transform your writing / Sarah L. Kaufman.
Description: New York: Penguin Press, 2026. | Includes bibliographical references.
Identifiers: LCCN 2025036173 (print) | LCCN 2025036174 (ebook) |
ISBN 9780593831465 hardcover | ISBN 9780593831472 ebook
Subjects: LCSH: Authorship—Style manuals |
English language—Verb | LCGFT: Style manuals
Classification: LCC PN147 .K37 2026 (print) | LCC PN147 (ebook)
LC record available at https://lccn.loc.gov/2025036173
LC ebook record available at https://lccn.loc.gov/2025036174

Printed in the United States of America
1st Printing

The authorized representative in the EU for product safety and compliance is Penguin Random House Ireland, Morrison Chambers, 32 Nassau Street, Dublin D02 YH68, Ireland, https://eu-contact.penguin.ie.

To John

vi. to make everything possible

Writing is: the science of the various blisses of language.

—ROLAND BARTHES

CONTENTS

PART II
THE POETIC

INTRODUCTION

Reporter: Senator Kennedy, do you agree with your fellow candidates that the president has mishandled the crisis in Afghanistan?

Ted Kennedy: Well, in this moment of national crisis, any second-guessing that I . . . er . . . personally, with respect to the interests of peace. Moreover, with the . . . uh . . . unchallenged Soviet threat, the . . . er . . . grain embargo which . . . uh . . . as far as strong leadership in this country! Now, in respect to the . . .

Reporter: A verb, Senator, we need a verb!

Verbs are the underrated stars of the English language. They hold it all together: sentences, imagery, meaning. A complete sentence cannot exist without one, yet a single verb can create complete meaning. (See?)

What's more, verbs unlock the infinite potential of written expression, propelling poetry, metaphor, and emotion.

Verbs, as we learned in grade school, are action words, and they tell us about energy and states of being. These are formless and transitory conditions; maybe that's why many people tend not to think too much about verbs—about *defining* action with verbs. Nouns, the companions and ideas of our days, the things we see and touch, may surface first in the writer's mind. Yet writers who take little notice of verbs miss the electric effects of life, the flashes that excite and enliven. They can fall into lame and long-winded language. Like this: *It looked like a storm was coming so we decided to go home in a hurry.*

Vivid, dynamic verbs will not only energize your writing, they'll streamline it: *A storm loomed; we dashed home.* The scene jumps to life.

In the same way, action verbs can reveal subtle feelings, to show what's happening inside and out. Compare these:

A. Lena didn't want to seem like someone who was easily flustered so she tried to make herself look confident.

B. To hide her jitters, Lena steeled her spine and lifted her chin.

Fewer words, sharper picture.

Great writers understand the power of verbs. Let's start with F. Scott Fitzgerald. His masterpiece, *The Great Gatsby*, is a profoundly poetic novel of forty-seven thousand words. The final fourteen throw the knockout punch—and they're among the greatest last words in literature—because of the verbs:

> So we beat on, boats against the current, borne back ceaselessly into the past.

With that sentence, Fitzgerald releases his readers under a delicate spell of emotion and sensation: wistfulness, melancholy, a pining sting. Dogged optimism despite the strikes against it. The feeling—the magic—springs from Fitzgerald's choice of verbs.

"So we beat on," "borne back . . ." You might feel his verbs in your body, so delicately you're not quite aware of it. The repeated *B* sound—beat, boats, borne back—is percussive. The physical resonance of the verb *beat* may echo internally in many ways, as you feel a soft drumbeat, as your heart beats. Reading "borne back" may light a brief, indistinct flickering inside, a sense of how your own consciousness can whoosh backward in time.

Verbs can leap off the page and land in our bodies. They tickle the senses. They delight the instinct for movement. At times, they may tell you something true about yourself. All that in a word.

Fitzgerald mastered verb use: He wielded the emotional and sensual power of verbs to make us feel. In his closing sentence, the verbless phrases "boats against the current" and "ceaselessly into the past" carry the theme of *The Great Gatsby*: the inescapable drive of our deepest yearning, and the futility of resurrecting a long-ago love affair. But the verbs, with their meaningful energy, burn the ineffable poignancy of that theme into our hearts.

If Fitzgerald had chosen common, humdrum verbs, his last line wouldn't hit us physically and emotionally with the same force. Say, for instance, he'd written: *So we carry on, boats against the current, sent back ceaselessly into the past.*

Rather sticky, isn't it? All stops and starts, caramel in the teeth. It conveys roughly the same idea, that we may think we're moving forward but we're entangled with our histories. The sentence won't linger in memory, though. "Carry on" is tuneless, so expected it's almost flippant. It doesn't dovetail with "boats against the current." And "sent back"? That's the fate of misaddressed mail.

Fitzgerald's phrasing—driven by his verb use—strikes a sharper, clearer, and more dramatic emotional tone.

* * *

This book shines the spotlight on verbs—their fire, subtlety, and power.

Verbs ignite emotions, transform our thoughts, and stimulate our bodies. Embodied theories of language suggest that we understand verbs, at least in part, by mentally simulating how they feel in our bodies. (We'll explore some fascinating verb-related scientific discoveries in chapter 10.) Verbs cue movement images in our minds, and writers who use verbs well access the reader's imagination directly.

Precise, dynamic verbs bring stories to life and make accounts, reports, and other communication sharper and clearer. Yet many writers clutter their work with dull, imprecise verbs and too many adverbs, missing out on the crisp clarity of a great verb. They misuse verbs, ignore their potential, make boring choices. They waste opportunities to stir feelings and intensify themes.

In the following pages we'll analyze the brilliant and the bland. We'll look at how journalists and literary writers can animate scenes, landscapes, and characters with action verbs; how marketing and communications professionals can boost emotion and urgency with dynamic verbs; and how any writer can reveal personality and hidden truths through verbs. I'll show you examples from the news, literature, science texts, advertisements, websites, and more—writing that works and writing that doesn't, with discussions of the difference. And I'll give you tools to send your own prose soaring.

Verb Your Enthusiasm comprises a style manual and a philosophy of good writing. I'll be making the case—practically as well as poetically—that if you want people to know what you mean, you need accurate verbs. This book is not a grammar guide, though you'll find a grammar refresher in chapter 2, with a sharp focus on verbs. But I'm not interested in rules. I want to open your imagination.

My argument is simple: Excellent writing requires smart verb choice and thoughtful verb use. This is the best-kept secret of fine literature, award-winning journalism, and even persuasive marketing. But it's not only for professional writers. Verb mastery improves all writing—emails, copywriting, research papers, blog posts, fundraising appeals, poetry, fiction, or nonfiction prose. Dynamic verbs can make your writing sing. And striving for the most accurate verbs improves your thinking and helps you home in on what you want to say.

* * *

What you'll find here is a fresh, pragmatic way to explore the fundamentals of craft and style. Focusing on verb use leads naturally to a discussion of other elements of good writing. Clear thinking, for example. To choose just the right verb—one that expresses what you see in your mind, what you feel in your body, what you're driven to share—you must first deeply understand your subject, through curiosity, empathy, and observation. Then you can zero in, paring away jargon and cliché in favor of truth. The concentrated mind can more easily craft clear, coherent sentences, leading to a clean and elegant composition.

I've learned these lessons in more than thirty years as a journalist, most of them at *The Washington Post* as the chief dance critic and senior arts reporter. I began there as a copy editor while moonlighting as a dance writer—and this meant struggling to capture an ephemeral art through words. I leaned on verbs. When you think about it, dance is ephemeral because it is *all* verbs. It exists only as action, vanishing moment to moment, leaving no physical trace behind. It is all about change. A dancer leaps across the stage, nearly flying, and as I watch her, my heart knocks in excitement. What triggers that response, that sympathetic feeling of flight? How do I free the afterimage from my mind and explain it on the page? I discovered that generating verbs—hurtle, soar, plunge, rebound—helped my writing fall in place. Mulling the action words, I saw what mattered in the scene and felt my emotions anew.

That's why this is fundamentally a book about *you.* What feelings of drama or tension, exhilaration or peace, do you sense in the people and events you're writing about? I want to encourage you to notice and feel a world of action, emotion, turmoil, and change. A world that you alone can interpret for the rest of us—with well-chosen verbs.

I believe anyone can write, and it needn't be a struggle to turn out effective prose. I've taught writing throughout my journalism career, in Harvard's continuing education division and at Princeton, American University, the National Critics Institute, and more. I've guided undergraduates and professors, reporters and artists, lawyers and diplomats toward clearer, more elegant and persuasive writing. I always stress the power of verbs. When my students grasp how these little fireballs fuel good writing, their work improves.

I'll share my own writing experiences with you as we explore the great, radiant landscape of verbs. We'll grind passive verbs to dust, except where they're necessary. We'll use accurate verbs to banish clumsy, cluttering adverbs. We'll consider clever new verbs and discover how they flash to life, and who pushes them forth. (This might surprise you.) I'll also lead you through the latest science on how verbs stimulate our bodies and our brains and why they possess a unique ability to communicate meaning. Each chapter ends with a Good Habits section of tips and quick exercises that expand the chapter's themes. They'll deepen your understanding of the craft of writing. The appendix lists lively vintage verbs that deserve a comeback.

This is all in service to your passion, your desire to write and express yourself clearly, to connect with others through words and sentences brimming with character and grace. Sentences that convey just the right spirit and intent.

Let's verb your enthusiasm and make your readers feel it, too.

PART I

THE PRACTICAL

CHAPTER 1

Energize

Discover why verbs are the secret superpower of language. Learn how precise, dynamic verbs add muscle, clarity, passion, and truth.

> As soon as Kira caught sight of him, she leaped for the door and zoomed out—like a rocket! Whoosh!
>
> —WINIFRED AND CECIL LUBELL

Propped near my desk sits the first book I ever devoured cover to cover. Truly devoured; several pages bear marks of my early habit of chewing on the corners. I'm sentimental about such things. When I was in kindergarten, I read this slender book, titled *Up a Tree*, to my classmates, with the teacher holding it for me, the page-turner to my little étude. I was a shy child who avoided drawing attention; still, I'd never felt so confident as I did that day, holding forth on the antics of a cat named Kira. The book describes her outdoor adventure that begins when a neighbor's dog bursts into the house, and Kira zooms out her little cat door with the dog racing after her.

My five-year-old psyche zoomed with her. That instant escape thrilled me—it still does, to be honest. *Up a Tree*, by artist and writer Winifred Lubell and her husband, Cecil, a literary scholar, brims with bright, vigorous verbs: *chased, dashed, rushing, running,* "yowling her head off." Of course, as a children's book it's striving to keep beginning readers' attention, and the upbeat action helps. I like to think the fast-paced narrative ignited my passion for capturing action in words.

That's what *Verb Your Enthusiasm* is about, in a nutshell: learning to express action and change, whether bold or quiet, on the page.

I have relied on the power of verbs every day of my career. I started out as a copy editor for various newspapers, fixing blundered syntax and writing verb-centered headlines. On the race-day status of a horse with hives: "Rash May Scratch Alysheba." (Two thoughts spring to mind: That example dates me. And we all could have wept when the edict came down to stop punning the headlines.)

Eventually I landed at *The Washington Post* and shifted to writing. I poured years of ballet and tap lessons and everything I'd learned from a college job at a ballet school into nearly three decades as a dance critic. Night after night I had the world's best sight lines onto the most extraordinary athletes of the stage: pliant ballerinas, gallant romantics, quicksilver tappers, experimental shapeshifters. Flamenco dancers, their heels hammering like hail. To watch these artists move was to hear their hearts speak.

As a young critic, this worried me.

How could I possibly interpret this dynamic, wordless poetry in . . . words? These amazing human beings spin miracles out of music, sweat, and thin air. Their poetry appears and disappears with every step. To write something truthful about a live art—well, to me that seemed about as easy as strutting onstage to pound out my own sevillana.

I found my confidence through verbs. When I write about dance, I seek to re-create the experience of being there, by painting an active portrait of the event and the spell it cast. The right verbs help. Initially, I didn't set out to make my mark through verbs, but I did try to make my writing interesting. I covered a rather niche field, after all, and I wanted to reach a wide audience. Verbs showed me the way. I found the means to think and write about vanishing things by choosing the most accurate, evocative verbs. For example, my last review in the *Post* focused on a dance by the marvelous Belgian Colombian choreographer Annabelle Lopez Ochoa. Her subject was Argentina's famous former First Lady. This is the opening paragraph:

> Eva Perón tears the shoes off her feet and hurls them into the wings. She shouts; she stamps; she flies into the arms of half a dozen lovers. She sprints around the stage trailing white silk like the luminous mist of her own star power.

The verbs I use are simple and blunt. Nothing fancy about them—and that's intentional. I chose short, descriptive verbs that drive the story. They speed it along, conveying, I hope, the energy of the dancer. Also, it's fun to shove aside plain-vanilla *leaps* and *turns* and instead describe people billowing and drifting across the stage, shuddering and scootching, soaring like shooting stars arcing into darkness. Closely observing action can spark all kinds of images, and getting one's descriptions rolling with dynamic verbs gives a writer the power to trigger the reader's imagination as well.

* * *

It's the classic rule of journalism: Honor the verb, sacrifice the adjective.

The reporter's aim—the aim of any serious writer—is to produce clean, honest, uncluttered prose. Novelists and poets, fact-finding reporters, executives, managers, students: Every writer must set high standards and strive for clarity and coherence. This is true whether the writing concerns fiction or fact, opinion or research.

As a reader, I also look for enthusiasm. What pulls me in is passion, warmth, and spirit. Throughout this book I'll share top-notch writing of all kinds, and what makes these works snap, sizzle, and catch my heart is enthusiasm—which the writers express with vivid verbs. Great writers honor the verb.

In the passage below from Sally Rooney's novel *Beautiful World, Where Are You*, a young woman writes to her friend about something rather abstract. She had been trying to reclaim the optimism of past years, she writes, and at last she experienced a sudden flash of it. Notice how Rooney takes us through her narrator's mental actions and then shifts to the actions of an unnameable emotion:

> As soon as I realized what I was feeling, I tried to move toward it in my thoughts, to reach out and handle it, but it only cooled a little or shrank away from me, or slipped off further ahead.

This sentence has the clean, flowing energy that Rooney is known for, thanks in large part to her choice of verbs. Simple verbs—*move*, *handle*, *cool*, *shrink*—hold down the slippery evanescence of thoughts and feelings, so we can see them (and feel them) from different perspectives, and understand something about them. Maybe the verbs prompt us to reflect on our own fleeting emotions, too. That's what they do to me. The writing swirls and flows and my own thoughts eddy along in rhythm.

The best verbs define intention and action, even subtle thinking action, with elegant simplicity. Let's take a quick look at various kinds of verbs now, because understanding the differences among verbs will help you choose what's best for what *you* mean to say. Making deliberate verb choices can sharpen your work.

Think of three piles. The first contains "stative verbs," which are all about a *state* of being rather than a dynamic action. They include *to be* and many other verbs—*appear*, *believe*, *know*, *love*, *prefer*, *un-*

derstand, and more—that describe a static situation such as existence, emotion, thought, or a condition.

The other piles comprise two different kinds of action verbs, which we'll call "basic verbs" and "verbs of manner."* A basic verb is neutral, ordinary: The dog *walks*. Verbs of manner are the drama queens, descriptive and specific: The dog *wiggles/waddles/wanders*. These verbs tell us the *way* in which an action happens, its speed, force, and feeling—its manner.

Verb-wise, if you write in English, guess what? It's your birthday every day—with shopping sprees at FAO Schwarz—because English overflows with verbs of manner. It's a special feature of the language. A secret superpower, in fact. Linguist Dan I. Slobin at the University of California, Berkeley, has studied verbs of manner around the world, and he notes that, for example, French and Spanish each have a single verb for a jumping motion (*bondir* in French, *saltar* in Spanish). But English? It boasts at least half a dozen: *jump* as well as *hop*, *leap*, *spring*, *bound*, and *bounce*. You can probably think of more.

Slobin estimates that French, Spanish, Turkish, and Hebrew have just a few dozen verbs of manner. English, however, has *several hundred*. (So do German, Dutch, Russian, and Hungarian.) Every language has unique features and advantages, and certainly English has its hitches (all those irregular verbs!). But with a great many verbs of manner at their fingertips, writers can express a specific action and energy with a single word. For example: "The road zigzags up the mountain." Lively, efficient. You'd have to use a few more words in other languages; in Spanish, for instance: *La carretera sube en zigzag por la montaña*. ("The road climbs in zigzags up the mountain.")

Take advantage of this deep verb vocabulary to find the exact verb that is accurate and truthful for your purposes. Verbs of manner can pop off the page—or, in this example, out of a character's mouth:

*Linguists also call them "manner-of-motion verbs"; I prefer the shorter term.

> All they do is chatter and bark and eat and the knives and forks click and clack and the words cut and the teeth snap and snarl. And in that place—*there*—will live my paintings for all time.
>
> —PAINTER MARK ROTHKO, IN JOHN LOGAN'S PLAY *RED*, RAILING ABOUT THE ATMOSPHERE AT A RESTAURANT THAT COMMISSIONED HIS WORK

Throughout Logan's play, Rothko roars with strong feelings, most of all the fear of being unappreciated and forgotten. In this scene he cloaks that fear with contempt—and aggressive verbs of manner. In the lines above, basic verbs would only sound flat and boring; to wit: "All they do is talk and eat and make noise with their cutlery and teeth. And my paintings will exist there."

You may not wish to use dramatic verbs of manner in every instance, however. It's not wise to do so willy-nilly. It's impossible to write anything coherent without basic verbs and stative verbs. Let's take another look at Sally Rooney, who uses basic verbs with artful intention:

> Alice came to their housewarming party, dropped a bottle of vodka on the kitchen tiles, told a very long anecdote about their college years which only Eileen and she herself seemed to find remotely funny, and then went home again.

Comings and goings, klutziness and ramblings—Rooney treats them evenly with basic, neutral verbs. There's fluid movement in this passage, making it lovely to read, but the tone is calm. Rooney's voice is intimate and natural. Her young lovers fall into affairs and misunderstandings, but she doesn't judge them.

Whether toned down, subtle, or bold, verbs can deliver tremendous expressive power. In the coming pages we'll explore how such a small word change as the verb—a *deceptively* small change, that is—heightens feeling and intent.

The right verb carries a whole world with it, like an actor transforming the stage:

> In the beginning God *created* the heavens and the earth.
>
> Friends, Romans, countrymen, *lend* me your ears.
>
> Just like me / they *long to be* / close to you.

Change the verb (or with *long to be*, the verb phrase) in any of these sentences and you sap their strength. As they are, they tell us everything. God is not only skilled and powerful but inventive, too. Shakespeare's Mark Antony wants us to believe that he's polite, undemanding, and not out to steal our time. He's also foreshadowing more ironies to come. And in Burt Bacharach and Hal David's song "(They Long to Be) Close to You," birds, stars, and all the girls in town are past wanting and wishing. They're gripped by desire.

The writers of those lines composed in simple subject-verb format ("God created"), with the subject and verb close together, at or near the beginning of the sentence. This gets meaning across in the clearest and most energetic way, because *the verb contains the meaning*. What a productive thing, the choice verb! Find that verb and allow your voice to emerge.

* * *

Even advertising turns poetic with a potent verb. A jeweler's website I stumbled upon described its turquoise as having "slipped from the sky."

No ordinary stones, these. There's a sense of magic in "slipped from the sky." Destiny, too. Navajo tradition holds that turquoise descended from the heavens. *Slipped* echoes this belief. It carries a hint of spiritual intent, as if the stone meant to ease itself free, silent and imperceptible. It didn't just succumb to gravity and fall, like . . . well, like a rock. A mineral that slips won't crash to earth. I imagine it gliding to rest. More mystery, less geology. All in the choice of verb.

Starting your sentences with a subject and verb is wise, but that alone does not guarantee meaning. Your subject needs the *right* verb. Fuzzy, misused verbs confuse readers and stop them. Here's an example from a chamber of commerce website, promoting a gala dinner with pricey sponsorships:

> The annual meeting represents an evening of celebration, connection and recognition as the Chamber reflects on its accomplishments and shares its priorities for the year ahead.

The writer begins with a subject ("the annual meeting") and a verb ("represents") but the verb is wrong. The meeting *represents* an evening of celebration? So it's just a symbol of a celebration, not the real thing? Further on, "the Chamber reflects" is weak and vague. Watching a group "reflect" offers no reason to pony up thousands of dollars for a table.

The chamber's notice is like many press releases and marketing materials: dull, tiresome text that promises a dull, tiresome outcome. It swells with self-importance. Instead of muscular verbs—verbs with drive and energy—this writer used stodgy nouns derived from verbs (*celebration*, *connection*, *recognition*). Don't let your writing sink under the weight of such starch.

The right verbs, strong and clear, will add muscle to your work, as we'll see throughout this book. To grab their power in this example, speak directly to the reader about your goal. Name the actions you want to see. Assert your point with verbs:

> Join us to celebrate what we've achieved together. Connect with members as we reveal our plans.

That's sixteen words instead of the original twenty-six, and I've added *together* to stress this meeting's point: connecting. *That's* important. Important enough for careful writing.

Here's a line from a doctor's ad in a health magazine:

> Dietary intolerances are also common and can be addressed with a physician who is able to address them.

Would you make an appointment with this person? The ad offers no argument for doing so. It meanders in circles—"can be addressed with a physician who is able to address . . ." Yawn. Say it straight. "Dr. Fixit specializes in these."

Instead, this writer failed to convince and the doc failed to proofread. Sloppy writing turns my thoughts to sloppy care.

Straight, honest verbs also improve everyday writing tasks—emails, reports, blog posts. We can all fall into habits of overwriting even the simplest points. Find the plain truth under the excess. Your reader, hacking through the overgrown jungle of her inbox, will thank you. For example:

> Our auction ~~will go live~~ *launches* at 9 a.m. ~~on~~ Sunday, April 30~~th~~. ~~Keep an eye out~~ *Watch* for the link in your inbox. We'll also ~~make the announcement~~ *announce it* on social media, so ~~make sure to~~ follow us here:

* * *

Clutter smothers meaning. One of the worst clutterers I've seen is the well-meaning government of my former hometown. For many years I lived in a neighborhood straddling a wooded creek that was home to an astonishing number of deer. They were a sociable bunch and liked to dine out, so they brought their children, cousins, aunts, and uncles into our yards for picnics and left few blooms behind. Each spring the neighborhood listserv lit up with outrage over deflowered perennials and disappearing greenery. Some folks favored managed deer hunts, others hotly opposed them. And what about ruminant birth control? Inevitably someone would ask the mayor to weigh in. Here's an excerpt from one of her office's email replies:

> It has been determined that current materials and methods included in immunocontraception and surgical sterilization efforts are not suitable for use as a means to directly reduce deer numbers on the large scale, widespread and high deer density park areas of the county. While we remain open to the possibility of one day employing the use of non-lethal methods for managing deer populations, we recognize that current limitations and constraints will not allow for practical, cost effective, and sustainable management using these tools as they exist at present.

I couldn't make that up if I tried. Did the writer get paid by the word? The statement boils down to this:

> Birth control methods won't work right now to limit deer numbers in the most deer-heavy parts of the county. Maybe one day we won't have to kill the deer to control the population but we're not there yet.

And the other way? So much taxpayer-funded time, so little coherence.

* * *

Well-chosen verbs help readers grasp the essence of your subject. Verbs can reveal the nuances, color, tone, feel, style, and look of even the smallest action. They can convey a distinct, detailed personality.

Let's look at how award-winning reporter Eli Saslow uses verbs to capture a character at the beginning of this *Washington Post* article:

WAITING FOR THE 8TH

THE MONTHS SEEM A BIT LONGER FOR A D.C. WOMAN AND HER FAMILY AFTER RECENT CUTS TO THE FOOD STAMPS THEY RELY ON.

> She believed you could be poor without appearing poor, so Raphael Richmond, 41, attached her eyelash extensions, straightened her auburn wig and sprayed her neck with perfume as she reached for another cigarette. "For my nerves," she explained, even though doctors already had written eight prescriptions to help her combat the wears of stress. She blew smoke into the living room and waited until her eldest daughter, Tiara, 22, descended the stairs in new sneakers and a flat-brimmed baseball cap.
>
> "I look okay?" Tiara asked.
>
> "Fresh and proper," Raphael said, and then they left to stand in line for boxes of donated food and day-old bread.

Saslow, who's now a writer at large for *The New York Times*, specializes in untangling complicated subjects. In 2014, as a national reporter at the *Post*, he won his first of two Pulitzer Prizes for telling

Raphael's story and others in a series about the sharp rise in the number of Americans who depend on the federal food stamp program. The drive in Saslow's writing springs not from lengthy, adjective-heavy description but from verbs. Much of the empathy, too.

Note how quickly Saslow establishes an intimate connection to his main character. He achieves this by taking us into her mental state. He begins with a subject and a verb: "She believed." Not "What you need to know about Raphael Richmond is this . . ." or "Getting dressed up was important to Raphael Richmond, even though . . ." or the standard dull introduction: "Raphael Richmond, a 41-year-old mother of two, . . ." No describing here, no explaining, just a declarative subject-verb statement, clear and strong.

Get to the point with a simple subject-verb structure.

Why open the story that way? To establish Raphael's mindset as essential, the most important thing to know about her. This belief drives her actions. That force of will—not wanting to look poor—governs the entire passage and gives it poignancy and warmth. But Saslow doesn't waste time explaining that either.

Like a filmmaker, he pulls back the camera and shows us Raphael in crisp phrases built on four verbs: *attached, straightened, sprayed, reached.* These actions demonstrate Raphael's perfectionism and self-respect, and the work she puts into pulling herself together. Here's a shining example of the power verbs have to convey energy, personality, and truth when a writer chooses with precision. Saslow's astute verb choices reveal core truths about this dignified woman who dresses in her Sunday best to stand in a breadline.

Speaking of that, Saslow's construction, from his first sentence on, sets us up for a punch. The verb phrase at the end of that passage, *to stand in line* for donated food and day-old bread, knocks the wind out of you, doesn't it? The surprise and poignancy of it. This is where Raphael's core belief and her preparations are leading her.

The reporter shows us the price she pays by invoking her doctors and their actions to help manage anxiety so formidable it must be *combated.* That verb underscores poverty's invisible, psychic peril.

From the first line, Saslow creates a dramatic scene, full of tension, activity, and emotion, and he does it with maximum economy. We don't need adverbs to help us understand that Raphael is nervous as she's smoking, or that her daughter is uncertain about her outfit.

Also, Saslow attributes their quotes with the simple verbs *asked* and *said*, rather than, for example, *inquired* or *responded.* This keeps the focus on the women's words, not his. Their speech and actions show us everything.

They tell the story.

* * *

Writing this way changes your perspective. Try placing your readers into a scene so they can hear, see, and feel it, and come to their own understanding. By showing readers a sequence of continuous action, you allow them to feel what it's like to be so close to people you can smell their cologne and grasp the thoughts and feelings behind their behavior. There's a sense of objectivity in Saslow's writing; he shows us what's happening without comment. But many of his verbs do tell us about his thinking, how he understands Raphael and her life. You see this, for example, in "She believed," and in his mention of combating stress. Saslow's work is fundamentally a call to empathy and understanding because he reveals meaning through people's actions. In this case, Raphael's efforts to gather herself and calm her nerves, told with powerful verbs, show the devastating effects of living on food stamps—effects that the officials who control her fate can't see. Her actions make clear the toll on her spirit. Saslow's clear, direct writing makes us care.

He undoubtedly saw other things while he sat with Raphael. Maybe she poked around in her handbag or gazed out a window. But as Mark Twain wrote: "The more you explain it, the more I don't understand it." The reporter doesn't need to give us every single detail; he focuses on a few telling actions that support his theme. When writers understand a moment well—seizing what it means, the story it tells—they can pare it to the essentials. They can cut the clutter.

But first, writers have to be there, be present—if not physically, then through careful listening and other means of perception.

Tune in to your senses, feel the pang of recognition.

* * *

Physical actions, conflict, high drama: These aren't the only events for vivid verbs. What about internal thought-action? Secret responses, flashes of memory, the leaps from feeling to feeling? With no outward action to speak of, these swirling internal states can generate excitement, revelations, and drama of their own.

One of Virginia Woolf's innovations was to turn her novelist's imagination to the quiet, hidden storms of the heart, and convey them with subtlety and simplicity. In her stream-of-consciousness narrative *Mrs Dalloway*, Woolf takes this to the extreme. Adopting the perspectives of several characters over the course of a single day, she uncorks the flow of impressions within them. What these people do isn't nearly as fascinating as what they *think*.

Here, Clarissa, the wife of a member of Parliament, tries to keep her cool during a surprise visit from her former lover, Peter, who has interrupted her sewing:

> "Do you remember the lake?" she said, in an abrupt voice, under the pressure of an emotion which caught her heart, made the muscles of her throat stiff, and contracted her lips in a spasm as she said "lake." For she was a child, throwing bread to the ducks, between her parents, and at the same time a grown woman coming to her parents who stood by the lake, holding her life in her arms which, as she neared them, grew larger and larger in her arms, until it became a whole life, a complete life, which she put down by them and said, "This is what I have made of it! This!" And what had she made of it? What, indeed? sitting there sewing this morning with Peter.

Woolf doesn't tell us what emotion Clarissa is feeling. It has no name, only felt action, in the true sense of emotion. The word *emotion* derives from the Latin word *movere*, to move—just as *motion* does. And *exmovere* (or *emovere*) means to move *out* or agitate. True to its etymology, emotion is a state of physical disturbances and stirrings: the racing pulse of passion, the stammering of nervousness.

Clarissa's physical sensations swell from tiny tightnesses to a full-body experience of morphing age, pride, and doubt. Do these verbs—*caught* (her heart), *contracted* (her lips)—trigger your own simulations, a sympathetic clutch in the chest, perhaps? Reading this passage, you might picture Clarissa's reactions or even feel something close to what Woolf describes. That's because Woolf excels at showing instead of telling.

As a writer, you'll spark a stronger emotional response in your reader when you forge past telling readers what your characters are feeling—saying they feel awkward, terrified, etc.—and, instead, show them blurting out inanities or vaulting across a woodland trail when a snake slips from the brush. Woolf doesn't tell us that Clarissa feels mixed up—she shows us, through motion verbs, the sensory experience of a bloated and unimpressive life. She unlocks Clarissa's secrets by dropping us into her body, where small muscles rage, memories fleshify and overlay the present, and time swings. Metaphorical images dance through Clarissa's mind: "*holding* her life in her arms"; it grows and becomes "a whole life, a complete life, which she *put down* by them . . ."

Writing about action isn't limited to the crisis you can see. Sometimes the most revealing action comes from within.

We'll explore this more deeply in chapter 6, on verbs and the power of suggestion.

* * *

Good Habits

First, find a notebook, any kind you like. You can also use a notes app on your phone and set up a file for verbs—I do this—but I also keep a notebook with me for random jotting and working out ideas. Use either method for any writing from these exercises, and for lists I'll suggest in later chapters.

Look at a paragraph or two in an article, email, or blog post. Spot the verbs of manner and basic verbs. Basic verbs are neutral, generic, such as *do, get, make, go.* Verbs of manner are more precise, offering defined action.

For example, compare these:

A. We made reference to our model building and were able to get it approved.
B. The client approved our model.

Drop a precise, active verb into a simple subject-verb sentence, and gain strength and power.

Try this with the passage you've chosen. After noticing the basic and manner verbs, see if you can tighten and improve the writing by replacing vague verbs with specific ones. Rewrite in sentences beginning with a subject and verb. See how many words you save.

From this bare-bones result, play around with adding an adjective or two to create a more fluid and appealing passage.

Now examine a short piece of your own writing—a page of fiction, journal entry, school assignment, news article, or marketing campaign—and highlight the verbs. Replace any vague verb with a similar one that's sharp and dynamic. Notice how these changes alter the tone and energy of your text.

CHAPTER 2

Curate

A grammar brushup on the versatility of verbs.

I am still studying verbs and the mystery of how they connect nouns. I am more suspicious of adjectives than at any other time in all my born days.

—CARL SANDBURG

The sculptor Richard Serra created enormous blunt works in metal. The steel hulls of ships inspired him, the ones he'd seen in the San Francisco shipyard where his father worked. Indeed, some of Serra's sculptures—rusty steel walls looming over parks or plazas—are the size of superyachts. But weighty as they are, and though they are anchored to the ground, they seem to be moving, tilting off axis or lengthening to the horizon.

They also invite *our* movement. We want to pass between their slabs, navigate their curvy passageways.

In Serra's obituary, *New York Times* art critic Roberta Smith pointed out that double action:

> But if these massive forms had a mystical effect, it came not from religious belief but from the distortions of space created

> by their leaning, curving or circling walls and the frankness of their materials.
>
> This was something new in sculpture; a flowing, circling geometry that had to be moved through and around.

To express the sense of continuous motion in Serra's works, Smith fills her writing with motion words: *leaning, curving, circling, flowing.* But those *-ing* words aren't verbs, not exactly. They're called participles, and though they're formed from verbs, they function as adjectives. Abuzz with the vitality of their verb roots, they modify, or describe, nouns, and they tend to do so with punch because they are so economical. They embody the rich expressiveness of verbs.

Verbs can be the most important words in a sentence, as we've seen. That's how they got their name, in fact. The word *verb* comes from the Latin *verbum*, meaning "a word." The action/state-of-being class of words earned that elemental name because the verb is so essential. Yes, the verb swelled to such stature that it gobbled up the name given to *all words.*

And as we'll see in this chapter, the verb is also the most versatile part of speech in the English language.

To understand just how versatile, it helps to review a touch of grammar. But fear not: If the English classes of your youth haunt your memory as living death, I got you. What I'll serve forth here is a digestible reduction, practical rather than theoretical. This is not a grammar book, so I'm not delivering a full multicourse grammar banquet. We'll cover a few choice bits to give you a clearer understanding of how verbs and "verbals" can energize your writing—and then we'll dash on.

I. Parts of Speech

Verbs and nouns are two of the nine parts of speech. All words fall into one of these nine "parts" according to their function in a sentence. Nine parts, nine categories, nine buckets of words. They are:

1. Nouns
2. Pronouns
3. Adjectives
4. Verbs
5. Adverbs
6. Prepositions
7. Conjunctions
8. Articles
9. Interjections

A quick review of the parts of speech

1. A **noun** is a person, place, or thing: Homer Simpson, Lisbon, rhinoceros.
2. A **pronoun** is a kind of generic noun shorthand, substituting for a specific noun, usually on the second reference.

   Example: Jay Gatsby is an enigmatic figure **who** hides **his** past.

Who and *his* are pronouns. Pronouns include *he/him/his*, *she/her/hers*, *it/its*, *they/them/theirs*, and additional gender-neutral or nonbinary pronouns such as *sie/hir*, *xe/xem*, *ze/zim*, etc. Pronouns come in other varieties, such as reflexive (*myself, itself*), relative (*who, whose, which*), demonstrative (*this, that, those*), and indefinite (*all, everybody, nobody, someone*).

3. An **adjective** modifies, or describes, a noun or pronoun.
   Examples: red, furry, lipstick-stained
4. A **verb** expresses physical or mental action or existence.
   Examples: see, believe, become
5. An **adverb** modifies, or describes, a verb, and can also describe an adjective or another adverb. It tells how and when something happens.
   Examples: quickly, quietly, never, often, very
6. A **preposition** shows the relationship between nouns/pronouns and other words. It describes relationships of direction, time, and role.
   Examples: over, under, before, among
7. A **conjunction** connects words and phrases in a sentence.
   Examples: and, but, so
8. An **article** is a small but mighty word that goes in front of most nouns to show specificity and quantity. Small as they are, articles are essential for proper syntax.
   Examples: a, an, the
9. An **interjection** interjects. It's a spontaneous emotional reaction, often with an exclamation point.
   Examples: hey, oh, whoops, wow, ouch

Okay! To sum up, here's a quick demo. The nine parts of speech can all live in one sentence. For example:

II. Verb Forms (also called verbals—adorable, no?)

I rely here as elsewhere in this book on *Webster's New World College Dictionary* and merriam-webster.com.

1. **Infinitive:** the pure, unchanged verb, preceded by *to*. The name is poetic, pointing to the infinite, indefinite quality of a verb when it does not specify person, number, or tense.
   Examples: to eat, to pray, to love

We'll look at the following verb forms in more detail in the next few pages; for now, here are general definitions:

2. **Participle:** a verb form that has some functions of both verb and adjective, ending in *-ing* or *-ed*.
   Example: They spoke with refreshing honesty.
   (The descriptive term *refreshing* carries the splash of "to refresh.")
3. **Gerund:** the present participle of a verb that acts as a noun—such as *writing*—where the word refers to the general action. But it retains certain characteristics of a verb. A gerund, unlike a noun, may take an adverb. Gerunds also often end in *-ing*.
   Example: Writing helped Ben work through his fears. Writing well helped Ben even more.
4. **Verbal noun:** a noun formed from a verb. Not all verbal nouns end in *-ing*, but some do.
   Example with *writing* as a verbal noun: "But now, though the writing might strike me as more beautiful than ever, I cannot read it without uneasiness," notes Sigrid Nunez in her novel *The Friend*, reflecting on Rainer Maria Rilke's *Letters to a Young Poet*. Compare with *writing* in the gerund

example above. Here, Nunez is not referring to the action or process of writing, but to writing as a thing—the material produced by means of the verb. Writing (gerund) produces writing (verbal noun).

FUN FACTS ABOUT VERBS

- Nouns can be reduced to pronouns, but verbs can't be reduced that way. A close equivalent is *does* (or *did*), as in "Brad likes to read before bed. Parker does, too."
- Some verbs pair with a little particle—a preposition or adverb—to form a new verb with a different meaning. These verb synergies are called "phrasal verbs." Examples: *call off* (a wedding), *bring up* (a child), *fire back* (at a gibe).
- Grammarians have different ways of classifying verbs. For our purposes, these are the main types of verbs: *linking, transitive,* and *intransitive.* Their differences depend on whether they take an object or "complement," or can stand alone.

  Linking verbs connect the subject to a complement, which is a word or phrase that enhances the subject or describes it. Example: That cheese was too mild for my taste. *Was* is the linking verb; *too mild* is the complement that describes the subject, *cheese*. Cheese = too mild. *Was* is the link.

  A *transitive verb* is one that you actively *do to something* or someone. It must have a direct object, a thing that receives the action. A transitive verb *needs to transit over* to a direct object. Example: She mails a letter every day. As a sentence,

She mails makes no sense on its own, because the action is incomplete without its direct object. She mails *what*? A letter. *Letter* is the direct object, the thing that completes the transitive verb.

An *intransitive verb* expresses a complete action, no direct object needed. No transiting. Example: The lion roars every evening. You can shorten it to: The lion roars. No need to ask, *What* does it roar? *Roar* is a complete action—and an intransitive verb.

Some verbs can be both. For example, the verb *leave*. Transitive: She left her phone in the locker room. (She left what? Her phone.) Intransitive: Bored and lonely, she left. (Complete action.)

- Verb tenses specify when an action occurs. They include *past* (we sailed), *present* (we sail), and *future* (we will sail); also *past perfect* (we had sailed), *present perfect* (we have sailed), and *future perfect* (we will have sailed).
- In addition to tense, verbs also have what's known as "aspect." Aspect gives us more context. It tells us about the action's duration. Most of us don't realize we're using aspect; it's folded into most past and present verb tenses, like a silent partner. In its "imperfective" forms, aspect adds a subtle sense of flow and motion. Though some grammar sources insist on four categories, it's easiest to think of aspect in two, perfective and imperfective. Here are some examples:

  Perfective aspect (verb + *ed*) signifies the action has ended: Kendall *has walked* all day / She *had walked* that route many times / She *will have walked* for miles.

Imperfective aspect (verb + *ing*) describes continuous or repeated action: Kendall *is walking* / She *was walking* / She *had been walking*. The action is more open, ongoing. Use aspect to usher in a twist—or life's deepest questions—when you pair it with another action that yanks the sentence in a new direction. For example:

> A few days later, Manjula *was cutting* vegetables when an unexpected thought *struck* her: "What am I? What is the purpose of being? How can any human being ever be doing nothing?" [Italics are mine.]
>
> —SUJATHA GIDLA,
> *ANTS AMONG ELEPHANTS: AN UNTOUCHABLE FAMILY AND THE MAKING OF MODERN INDIA*

The point of it all

Verbs are flexible, shape-shifting, fascinating all-arounders that take on different roles—action word, adjective, or noun—with grace and energy. They are the Cate Blanchetts of language. And they produce creative magic in the hands of a writer who knows how to use them. A writer, my friend, like you.

* * *

Now, for a closer look at the verb forms.

Participles

Participles are **verbs turned into adjectives**. They can perk up your writing with spirit and movement.

We use participles all the time: That's *stunning* news. What an *amazing* outfit. They fall in place with a reflexive rhythm. But do they, in fact, describe things that stun and amaze? Or, in casual use, have those words lost meaning? Within your imagination lie fresher verbs to turn into participles with expressive power. Take a look at one of Fitzgerald's pithy participial phrases in *The Great Gatsby*, which sets the scene of New York City's oppressive heat and din:

> *Roaring* noon. In a well-fanned Forty-second Street cellar I met Gatsby for lunch.

Participles come in two flavors, present and past. Present participles end in *-ing*. Past participles end in *-ed* or, when derived from an irregular verb, they take that verb's past tense. See how the participles inject action and emotion into these sentences:

Present participle: Her kindness eased my *gnawing* grievance.

(*Gnawing* modifies *grievance*, and conveys the sense of a grievance that eats away at a person, never letting up—it is happening in the present—the way a dog gnaws at a bone.)

Past participle: Sparky broke out of his cage, so run if you see *gnawed* bones.

(*Gnawed* modifies *bones*. Sparky might have munched up those bones—and may be coming for yours . . .)

Present participle: A swarm of *stinging* insects can ruin a picnic.

Past participle (irregular): Her *stung* skin blistered like road tar in August.

In Flannery O'Connor's short story "The Enduring Chill," a struggling young writer named Asbury suffers a strange illness and drags himself home to his mother's care. The story, to some extent, is autobiographical. O'Connor herself lived with lupus and she wrestled, as Asbury does, with the meaning of her pain and faltering hopes of deliverance through her religious faith. In the passage below, she exposes the workings of Asbury's mind as he lies in bed mulling the news that his illness isn't fatal after all. O'Connor caps his thoughts with a couple of choice participles:

> He waited the coming of the new. It was then that he felt the beginning of a chill, a chill so peculiar, so light, that it was like a warm ripple across a deeper sea of cold. His breath came short. The fierce bird which through the years of his childhood and the days of his illness had been poised over his head, waiting mysteriously, appeared all at once in motion. Asbury blanched and the last film of illusion was torn as if by a whirlwind from his eyes. He saw that for the rest of his days, frail, racked, but *enduring*, he would live in the face of a *purifying* terror. [Italics are mine.]

O'Connor captures Asbury's revelation with lyrical specificity, moving from sense to sense: what he feels, what he sees (and imagines). In this way, we experience the particular temperature of the chill that comes over him, which is different from the icy cold of his fever, and we sense the violence and magnitude of his vision of the future. Notice her powerful verb phrase: "torn as if by a whirlwind." The whirling builds on the motion of a bird image on the ceiling, and all of a sudden it takes on a kind of magic realism.

Then, with the participles *enduring* and *purifying*, O'Connor expands Asbury's vision to his whole existence. Both words have religious connotations that suit the supernatural feel of this scene. They also capture the tension of Asbury's insight. He'll live, but in pain; the fear of death will haunt him but might possibly elevate him. What a magnificent, suggestive use of a participle, "purifying terror." Is a terror that purifies a spiritual salvation? Will it bleach away Asbury's disappointments? Or will it further traumatize?

What's important to note here:

O'Connor controls and coordinates all her images. The sea, the whirlwind, a bird's flight, a sudden insight.

Her language is fresh; no clichés.

And she uses good, strong verbs and verbals that convey movement, drive—and mystery.

A writer's objective, particularly in a work of fiction, may not be to solve every puzzle, nor to make things rational and understandable in every instance. Even then, it's essential to choose just the right verbs for the objective. O'Connor does that here, deepening the creeping darkness.

* * *

Gerunds

Gerunds are **verbs used as nouns**. They refer to general actions or ideas: the idea of swimming, swiping, stampeding, etc. They may look like participles, because both verb forms often end in *-ing*, but there's a big difference: Gerunds behave as things.

However, because a gerund still retains some characteristics of a verb, it cannot be modified by an adjective, or preceded by an article. (Those belong to standard nouns.) Like other verbs, a gerund is modified by an adverb.

You can't make an omelet without *breaking* some eggs.

This refers to the general action or process of breaking eggs. *Breaking*, though, is quite different from a standard noun. It's still closely related to a verb, as is clear when I add an adverb and the sentence remains grammatically correct:

You can't make an omelet without *messily* breaking some eggs.

* * *

Verbal nouns

As the name implies, a verbal noun is **a noun formed from a verb**. It is in every respect a noun, but it can contain to some extent the echo and vibration of the verb root.

A verbal noun can be modified by an adjective, just like any noun, and it can take a determiner—such as an article (*a, the*), a possessive (*my, their*), or a number.

> Through the day, while *the baking* and *washing* and *ironing* were going on, the father lay and looked up at the roof beams. [Italics are mine.]
>
> —WILLA CATHER, *O PIONEERS!*

The baking, the washing, the ironing—all verbal nouns. Like other nouns, they can be preceded by determiners and described by adjectives, for example: How I love Jesse's expert baking! Don't forget to hang up the damp washing. The scorched dinners, the scorched ironing—I was pretty tired of my cousin's efforts to help.

Wallace Stevens uses a verbal noun with a determiner—a possessive—in one of his best-known poems, "Peter Quince at the Clavier":

> The body dies; the body's beauty lives.
> So evenings die, in their green *going*,
> A wave, interminably flowing. [Italics are mine.]

Stevens was fascinated by the tension between reality and the poet's imagination. "Their green going" wavers between both with a sense of motion and poignancy as it floats along with the other metaphors for nightfall and death. Beauty, though it may be abused and destroyed, is also part of the natural cycle—an idea whose complications Stevens explores with evident irony throughout the poem.

The title of Shirley Jackson's gothic novel *The Haunting of Hill House* (and the Netflix series it inspired) is a verbal noun, as are the horror-movie versions with titles shortened to *The Haunting*. With *-ing* at the end, the verb for a specter's continual, unwelcome visits becomes a noun, but it hints at action. A haunting may be a vague, mystical thing, but it retains the vigor of the verb.

While we're on the subject of titles, *The Awakening*—the name of Kate Chopin's early feminist novel—is also a verbal noun, as is *The Shining*—the title of Stephen King's opus—and so many others. Isolated verbal nouns like these, with a definite article, make splendid titles because they evoke action as well as mystery. They prompt us to ask, what *is* a haunting, an awakening, a shining? The words are at once familiar—we recognize the verb—and unfamiliar in a tantalizing way, because now that the verb is solidified, in effect, it is less distinct. We have to construct its meaning by imagining the verb as an experience, not just a single action. It implies a process.

Thinking about a haunting pulls me back to the creepy night I spent in a bed-and-breakfast that had a mysterious, romantic air even before I heard something scratching above the ceiling of my bedroom. I remember feeling unsettled as wind shook the windows. A rattling branch was making the noise above me, wasn't it? Why, then, did it sound like something—someone—peeling away at the joists splinter by splinter? I wanted it to stop and wished I weren't alone. Close enough to a haunting, for sure.

Verbal nouns can offer punchy, quick economy. An *-ing* word can accomplish what a whole phrase might, as in this passage from *Manhattan Transfer* by John Dos Passos:

> In the brick houses and the dingy lamplight and the voices of a group of boys kidding and quarreling on the steps of a house

> opposite, in the regular firm tread of a policeman, he felt *a marching* like soldiers. [Italics are mine.]

How immediate the impact of "a marching." It's more powerful than "he felt the sensation of soldiers marching" or "he felt the heaviness of marching soldiers." With two words Dos Passos sends rhythmic footfalls into your mind and body like a solid thing, like the pounding (that's a verbal noun, too) that his narrator feels.

Yet in other instances, verbal nouns—those ending in *-ation*, for instance—can clutter and complicate where a simple infinitive is best. Compare these two sentences:

The poem reflects a desire for the deeper *exploration* of humanity's complex relationship with fear.

The poem reflects a desire *to study* humanity's relationship with fear.

The second one is tighter, easier to follow. Nouns ending in *-ation* are long and vague-sounding: *exploration*, *actualization*, *intellectualization*, *miniaturization* (ironic, no?), and so on. When you encounter one of these cloudy, multisyllable blobs, ask yourself: What short action verb can substitute? Swapping an infinitive ("to study") for the long-winded phrase "for the deeper exploration of" gives you a shorter, clearer statement. When you're reviewing your own writing, look for these and ax them.

Avoid other *-ation* verbal nouns such as these rusty anchors:

Symbolization means the use of symbols. So say "the use of symbols."

Conceptualization? I have read this vague term in more than a few student papers. Yet using it does not make anyone sound smart. A concept (rooted in the verb *conceive*) by definition is an abstract idea. It works best when tied down to something specific, as in the concept of democracy. But stretched into a verb meaning "to form a conceptual form," then stretched even thinner to mean "the process of forming a conceptual form"? Use the original noun: *concept.* Also try *idea*, *image*, or *picture.*

When you find yourself reaching for long, foggy *-ation* nouns, rewrite your sentence with the shortest, plainest words possible. Notice the difference in grace and clarity.

* * *

Nouns are our reality; verbs are our dreams.

I don't remember where I came across that statement, and I don't know who wrote it. But I've long pondered what it means.

In his poetic, poignant novel *In the Country of Men*, Hisham Matar tells the story of nine-year-old Suleiman, a boy growing up in a traumatized Libya after Muammar Gaddafi's coup. At one point he visits the ancient Roman city of Lepcis Magna, which for more than a thousand years lay buried near what is now Tripoli. "Scattered by the lapping sea," Matar writes, the unearthed ruins and empty piazza look alive:

> White-stone-cobbled streets—some heading toward the sea, others into the surrounding green desert—marched bravely into the rising sand that erased them.

A dream, of course. A dream of willpower animating stone, of strong, silent things surging toward trouble. One could guess that's how a man returning to scenes from his ruined youth might want to remember his community. Matar stirs our sympathies with verbals: surrounding desert, rising sand. Streets that march and head to sea. By such means we also empathize with the young narrator who feels a living force in these structures, not just sturdy but defiant, tearing themselves from the earth.

Dream and truth dance together in the writer's mind. They have to. Do we ever truly know what moves and motivates friends, strangers, animals, anything at all in the world around us—what motivates ourselves, for that matter? Our language of action arose to put sound, and then scribbles, to physical impulses that we felt and carried out long before we analyzed them. Even now our knowledge is not perfect. We cannot stop time to scrutinize, nor enter the past or another person's heart. We have imagination, and we have verbs.

In verbs we catch the flash of life. We tease impressions from the inexorable roll of time. We prove that we paid attention. Select them to express *what life feels like to you.* You saw a thing of wonder and felt something; you were there, witnessing what others missed. You waited for connections to slide into place, you spent time thinking about them—and you released this interlacing to the world.

* * *

Good Habits

Practice cutting the fat by rewriting the sentences below. Your goal is to make the main idea clearer. Try these steps:

1. Focus on a subject and verb.
2. Substitute active verbs.
3. Revise in any other ways to cut wordiness.

For example:

An investigation of the bakery's rat problem was undertaken after the Health Department received complaints from dozens of customers.

SUBJECT VERB

Revision: The **Health Department investigated** the bakery's rat problem after dozens of customers lodged complaints.

1. His expectation was to set sail as soon as the inheritance check from his parents came in.
2. Meeting the new delivery requirement necessitates the hiring of numbers of new employees by the main office.
3. The organization of all the different members of a campaign is a task that would prove daunting for any incoming leader.*

Find more examples of wordy, weighty sentences and revise them to zero in on the main idea. Reports about government and public policy are great places to start. Rearrange to focus on subject and verb, and edit to get to the point.

*See Notes for some possibilities.

CHAPTER 3

Take a Stand

Passive voice or active voice? On the morality of verbs and keeping your writing honest.

She longed for cutlasses, pistols, and brandy; she had to make do with coffee, and pencils, and verbs.

—PHILIP PULLMAN, *THE TIN PRINCESS*

I'm standing in a tobacco barn at a small state park in southern Maryland. One of the park's features is the plantation that once belonged to a Tidewater aristocrat; he'd been a general in the Revolutionary War and one of the state's governors. He ran a lucrative farming business here, which I'm reading about on a wall placard titled "Gentleman Planter."

Sandwiched into praise for the proprietor's devotion to his riverside acreage is this peculiar statement: "Labor was provided by more than fifty slaves."

Was provided? I read the text again, certain I've missed something, but I haven't. That's it—one backhanded mention, phrased like a nod to the sponsors. (It resembles the kind of thing you read in a press release: "Funding was provided by the Ford Foundation.") It's as if dozens and dozens of enslaved people made their services available to the good general out of the kindness of their hearts.

Typical passive-voice confusion, but unusually reckless.

All too often, the passive voice complicates writing, as you've undoubtedly heard before. But here's why I raise this example: It's a real-world case that forces us to confront the larger problems of the passive voice. It demonstrates how the passive voice, even well meant, can soft-pedal reality.

Let's break down what went wrong here in saying labor "was provided" by slaves. First comes the poor choice of verb. *Provide*, a positive word, implies that the provider willingly, even happily hands over a product or service. That's assuming the verb is used in the active voice, as in: A good parent provides stability and love. Organizations and people with some sort of means, whether tangible or spiritual, *provide*. Obviously, they have to be willing to give. You see the weirdness here.

Second, the writer uses the verb in the passive voice. In describing a slave plantation, the statement "labor was provided by" creates distance from the actual people in bondage. A clearer, more accurate statement: "More than fifty enslaved people worked the farm." Compare that with "labor was provided by," which sounds detached and formal, a quality common to historical accounts. In this case it skews the circumstances, and creates a cascade of questions in the mind of a careful reader: Am I reading a puffery? What else does this wall text gloss over?

Plantation museums around the country are grappling with how to confront the traumatic national history of slavery, but this is not the way to do it, and the reason it jumps out at me is the *verb*. Both the verb and the voice of the verb crash against reality.

Let me be clear: I'm not out to banish the passive voice everywhere.

Good writers make smart choices, whether about specific verbs or the voice of their verbs. Let's look at those choices and delve into the various effects writers can achieve with both active *and* passive voices. By the end of this chapter, you'll have a clearer understanding of when to edit out the passive voice, when to use it, and how to do so effectively.

We'll start with the most serious mistakes—and who tends to make them.

But to make sure we're in tune so far, here's a quick refresher.

The voice of a verb tells you its relation to the subject of the sentence. When the subject of a sentence *performs the action*, it takes a verb in the active voice.

For example: I *made* a mistake.

> I = the subject, the one doing the action
>
> made = the verb, in the active voice

Clear and direct, right? I did a thing; I messed up and I'm taking responsibility. No excuses. Thank you, active voice.

But when the subject of a sentence *receives an action*, it takes a verb in the passive voice.

Like this: Mistakes *were made.*

> *Mistakes* = the subject, just lounging there like a docile Saint Bernard, not doing anything, just chilling
>
> *were made* = the verb, in the passive voice, because someone else is doing the making. The mistakes were made by . . . who knows?

"Mistakes were made" is the classic passive-voice example. The verb is passive indeed, letting whoever made those orphaned mistakes drop off the hook and slip away. Thanks to the passive voice, such shirking is grammatically possible, if spiritually exasperating. Text written in the passive voice can be more difficult to read because it's unemphatic. It tends to meander. It also minimizes those doing the action or removes them altogether.

Now, you may ask, what about the sentence "Mistakes were made by me"? That "by" phrase identifies the person doing the thing, doesn't it?

That's a sensible question. We read this type of construction—a thing *was done by* so-and-so—in journalism, history books, marketing reports, and narratives of all kinds. But remember: Adding "by me" or "by officials" or "by the crew of the *Titanic*" does not alter the verb, which remains in the passive voice (hooked up to a form of "to be"). And whoever did the action and made the mistakes is out of the spotlight, tacked onto the end.

It's a matter of emphasis.

In general, the active voice leads to writing that is clearer, simpler, and more assertive.

Passive voice: Intervention by the president *would not be welcome.*

Active voice: The president *should not intervene.*

Here's a passage I've condensed from the website history.com and rewritten in the passive voice (in italics):

> News about the 1918 influenza pandemic *was suppressed* in America and parts of Europe. In Spain, however, reporting *was freely published* on the illness in the press, which is how the world *was given* the false impression that the spread *was begun* in Spain. [forty-four words]

Now in the active voice:

> Wartime censors across America and parts of Europe *suppressed* news about the 1918 influenza pandemic. In Spain, how-

ever, the press freely *reported* on the illness, and so the world *gained* the false impression that the spread *had started* there. [thirty-nine words plus greater clarity on who hid the news]

Downplaying the "doer," withholding key information. This is why public officials say, "Mistakes were made." Oops, an error exists. Here I am saying something about it, so it's all good. And not my fault!

In 1973, Richard Nixon's press secretary Ron Ziegler declared that "mistakes were made in terms of comments," deflecting attention from his lies to *Washington Post* reporters Bob Woodward and Carl Bernstein in their Watergate stories. *The Atlantic* has published a list of politicians who have avoided full disclosure by saying "mistakes were made," including Vice President George H. W. Bush, referring to the Reagan administration's lies about the Iran-Contra scandal, and President Ronald Reagan, referring to the same thing.

When reporters asked President Clinton why the White House had invited a top financial regulator to a coffee for bankers who had donated to the Democratic Party, guess what he said? "Mistakes were made." Then he elaborated: "At the edges, errors are made, and when they're made, they need to be confessed and . . . we need to assume responsibility for them. And that's what I'm trying to do up here today."

Washington Post reporters John F. Harris and Peter Baker weren't buying that explanation for why his administration included a Treasury official at an event for political donors. "Clinton for the most part left unspecified the errors he had in mind," they wrote, "and his use of the passive-voice 'mistakes were made' phrasing left responsibility unassigned."

That's the trouble with the passive voice. It is often the enemy of clarity. It can create confusion. At its worst, it hides the truth.

* * *

Let's return to the plantation example. The passive voice can lead to problems in any context, but scholars have pinpointed it in works about race and ethnicity in particular. In a 2012 study of bestselling college textbooks on the subject, sociologist Kathleen J. Fitzgerald argues that the passive voice is a primary problem, and she cites such examples as: "Deportations *were launched*, in which illegal immigrants *were rounded up* and sent back to Mexico. Repatriations also took place, in which Mexicans, many of whom had been born in the United States, *were induced* to leave the country." (Italics are mine.)

"Time after time," Fitzgerald writes, "examples of historical racism are presented to the reader but the causal agents and perpetrators of this racism too often go unnamed."

Part of the appeal of the passive voice is detachment. It carries a whiff of the establishment, of secretive power and high-toned voices that never lose their composure even when describing cruelties and wrongs. Bombs were dropped, civilians were killed, hostages were taken. Australian documentary filmmaker and war reporter John Pilger put it this way: The passive voice can be "a weapon of discourse so those who committed terrible acts in the old empire could not be identified."

Writing in passive voice creates the sense of observing objectively from a distance. Bridging that distance is a grammatical act, but in many cases it must start as a philosophical one, or even a moral one.

This leads me to the morality of verbs. They tell us when someone is standing upright, shouldering responsibility and embracing vulnerability, and they also tell us when folks are ducking.

Verbs can reveal the truth or draw the curtain. This is why I emphasize that writers should think about their verbs, for we have responsibilities to our readers. They're spending time with our words, and they depend on us to provide meaning.

* * *

It's easy to fall into the clutches of passive voice. I've fallen into them myself.

One morning in my sophomore year at the University of Maryland, I walked into my Early Works of Shakespeare class just as the professor was handing back our research papers.

I still have my paper, a study of *Richard III*, blotted all over with Wite-Out in those pre-computer years. It was a labor of love showing a fair amount of strain: "Richard's purpose in marrying his rival's widow is never elucidated . . ." "The parallelism emphasized is noteworthy . . ."

Huh? *Who* doesn't elucidate? (A horrible, pretentious verb, by the way. I cringe.) *Who* emphasized? Could it be . . . that guy Shakespeare? The kind professor gave me an A, but she noted my use of abstractions and advised me, in her elegant handwriting, "to vary them with the simple expressions that lend clarity and grace to writing."

Clarity and grace. The twin peaks of the writer's quest. It occurs to me now that Professor Donawerth may have been channeling the smart, instructive *Style: Toward Clarity and Grace*, by Joseph M. Williams, published as a textbook a few years before. Without question, clarity and grace are the perfect expression of good writing, and I took her words to heart. In addition to her advice, she had clipped a hefty mimeographed article to my paper. Drawing on years of experience with overheated English majors, my professor knew the antidote to overwriting: George Orwell's classic 1946 essay, "Politics and the English Language."

She was right and he was right. He'll always be right. Orwell wrote his essay at a time of global tumult. World War II had ended with the atom bomb and a shattered Japan. The Soviet regime was rising. Violence was engulfing the Indian subcontinent as Great Britain puzzled out how to end its occupation. Orwell knew how swiftly human tragedy unspooled from corrupted speech and lies.

Foolish thoughts, he writes, lead to messy language. Flawed language fosters lazy thinking. Orwell rages against language perversions flowing from executives, academics, and politicians, who pollute everyday usage with inflated phrases, clichés, imprecisions, and jargon. A few years later, in his famous novel *1984*, Orwell would expand this argument, demonstrating how totalitarian governments can manipulate citizens with the misleading and euphemistic language of "Newspeak," created to limit free thought.

But there's good news, Orwell wrote in his essay. We can reverse the process: "If one gets rid of these habits, one can think more clearly."

Avoid the fancy phrases and pseudosophisticated fuzziness by adopting good habits. Notice the clutter and cut it away. Rewrite. Rewrite again, refining your work. You will find this helps you think more clearly, because you're forcing yourself to write what you really mean. (This takes patience.)

Orwell advises writers to steer clear of the passive voice. I agree—with certain reservations we'll look at in a moment.

In general, using too many verbs in the passive voice leads to:

1. more words,
2. stock phrases and tired constructions we've all heard before, and
3. clouded meaning, concealed motives, and a sense of insincerity.

* * *

Do these sound familiar?

> "It has been brought to our attention . . ."
>
> "The situation is being monitored . . ."
>
> "An investigation has been launched . . ."
>
> "Steps are being taken . . ."
>
> "Changes have been implemented . . ."

And don't forget:

> "As always, your feedback is appreciated."

Oh no. Do not give me that line and expect me to believe it.

We've all read these robotic, opaque non-messages before, in business or politics or anywhere people wish to look active and responsible without doing that work. Recall that passive-voice verbs don't only hide the doers; they remove them. This is why people avoiding responsibility lean on passive-voice verbs.

You may well ask: Who, by name, appreciates my feedback? Chances are that no one in a position to do anything about it appreciates it. I'm sorry. Not one person up there is doing the action of appreciating.

Logic exercise: Is the statement "Your feedback is appreciated" true or false?

Philosophy exercise: Does it matter?

It's likely that the memo has put us to sleep by the time that tagline appears. Blame the grab-and-go phrasing and the boring imprecision of the passive voice.

But rewrite that statement in the active voice and the warmth and tone improve. "We appreciate your feedback" feels more natural and personal. It sounds like an honest expression of gratitude, whereas "Your feedback is appreciated" sounds distant and cold—the voice of corporate auto-reply.

We read the passive voice all day long. No wonder so many of us end up using it. We live in a world where mortgage rates have been lowered or raised, lending products are subject to employment verification, all advertised offers are subject to change—and, by the way, don't bother to reply because the email address is not monitored for responses.

Not monitored by whom? Everyone and no one. We'll never know. The numbing chill of passive voice might as well come from Agent Smith, a dark suit with no personality and an earpiece.

The online agreements to which we must agree are always in the passive voice: *Your access privilege may be revoked, disciplinary action taken against you and/or appropriate legal actions may be initiated . . . The foregoing shall not be limited to incorporating promptly into your standard terms and conditions any language required by applicable law . . .* Clarity is not the point and the writers don't want us to know who they are.

We can take a tip from them, though. Passive voice is wordy. *Your* email recipient will thank you for limiting it. So will the instructor grading your paper and readers of your novel, essay, historical account, or blog post. They will applaud you for your economy of words, your clarity and freshness, and for using the active voice.

* * *

Writers ought to write what they mean. In some cases they need to take a point of view—a stand.

I learned to do this as a critic, but it wasn't easy.

"I can't tell whether you liked the show or not," an editor once protested after reading a review I'd written. I was a new hire at the time, and I vowed never to hear those words again. So I studied other critics. I noticed that the best ones wrote in the active voice and made clear, well-defined statements. You may know some of my favorites (if not, seek out their work and settle in for a good time): *The New Yorker*'s Pauline Kael (on movies) and Joan Acocella (on dance); the *Chicago Sun-Times*' great, plainspoken sage of the cinema, Roger Ebert; and the former *New York Times* theater critic Frank Rich. I admire their well-reasoned arguments—and I treasure the heat and passion of their language. Much of the energy comes from their verbs. Kael on *Funny Lady* (the sequel to Barbra Streisand's huge hit *Funny Girl*): It "crashes along for almost an hour and then it hits a failure point, from which it never recovers."

Here's Rich, on a revival of his favorite show: "'Gypsy' may be the only great Broadway musical that follows its audience through life's rough familial passages. . . . It speaks to you one way when you are a child, then chases after you to say something else when you've grown up." That's a verb-driven image to savor: a work of art so robust and alive that it *pursues* us with different messages through time.

In judging art, these critics insist on clear expression and meaningful ideas, and they inspired my own high standards. I also embraced their zest for connecting with readers. Good writing shines with the writer's warmth and enthusiasm, as I noted in chapter 1, and with the markings of a firm, lively mind—all elements that draw readers to her work.

Yet many writers, out of habit or inexperience, avoid taking a stand. Whether in a review, analysis, essay, column, or letter to the editor, some are afraid to say what they think, afraid to take responsibility or be judged. So they smudge things with the passive voice, blurring meaning with a thick smear of words. This frustrates readers and stops them from reading.

Here is an array of passive verbs in a well-meaning letter to the editor:

> During the meeting, no meaningful questions were asked by the Council. Details went by unchallenged. Assertions were made and left as fact. Revelations came to light and were left in darkness.

The tone is flat. Compare this rewrite:

> Did the Council ask meaningful questions? Did any member challenge the developer's details and assertions? No. The developer even alluded to problems. No one asked him to explain.

The passive voice has invaded colleges and universities, as I've seen in writing classes I've taught over the years. In these examples from students, I've given active-voice corrections after the slash:

- The importance of presentation that *is emphasized* in the scene . . . / In this scene, the director emphasizes . . . (and we need a specific noun here—personal style? ceremony?—rather than the fuzzy "presentation")
- More attention *is demanded to be paid* to the sport. / The sport demands more attention.
- Problems *have recently been illuminated* with the rise to prominence of . . . / After [blah blah] happened, problems arose.

I often see this blurring effect when I teach arts criticism or persuasive writing. Bravely reviewing a musical for the first time, one student wrote: "However, if this pace is to be considered an ailment of the play by some, it is rescued by the music and lyrics." *If it is to be considered* . . . Why does such overwrought vagueness come more easily to the inexperienced writer than simplicity? To me, it's because many folks mistake roundabout wordiness for sophistication. Yet indirectness often signals insecurity, cloaked in a muddle of words, and the fear of taking a position.

Your passion will make your work memorable. Let it come through. Say it straight.

Foggy, smushed-around writing can resemble those legal texts and government reports that brim with unnecessary complication. These should be clear and direct, too, and light on the passive verbs and redundancies, like all good writing. Their writers are either anonymous or, alas, forgettable. You don't want that fate.

I advised my student to concentrate on what she meant and write it down in plain words, with a subject and a verb in the active voice. Her result: "The pace is slow at times, but the music and lyrics make up for it."

Brava.

* * *

Active-voice verbs tell us who does what. They make the chain of activity clear. But active construction alone does not guarantee good writing or fresh expression.

Example: Simone Biles takes gymnastics to the next level.

Subject: one of the world's greatest athletes. Subject + verb + object: Simone Biles takes gymnastics . . . Direct and active. So far so good.

But wait: She takes gymnastics *where*? What does "take to the next level" mean here? It's a cliché. A waste of space! Sure, we can guess that it gestures vaguely at the difficulty of her moves, the height and power she achieves, or her innovations in the sport. But why make readers guess, when a clear statement is much more useful to them—and more intellectually satisfying for the writer?

Plenty of poor writing contains the active voice. Overused phrases with active verbs litter our discourse. There's "taking it to the next level" as well as "paving the way for," "proves unsurprising," and the like.

In the infinite arena of language choices, these snoozers race to the expensive seats and jostle for attention. The writer aiming for vigor, clarity, and freshness must ignore them and reach higher. Orwell, in "Politics and the English Language," warned against an "invasion of one's mind by ready-made phrases." He cited as examples the verb phrases "lay the foundations" and "achieve a radical transformation." (Note that both use active-voice construction.) The invasion of these phrases "can only be prevented if one is constantly on guard against them," Orwell wrote, "and every such phrase anesthetizes a portion of one's brain."

He knew the chances of victory were low, and he was right. "Lay the foundations" is ever popular. My search of scholarly literature over the past five years turned up more than seventeen thousand instances, including this, in a recent music journal: "To lay the foundations for lifelong musical practices, parents need to feel confident using music as a part of their everyday parenting."

And what will be the result if they do? It's better to help parents

When words clump in your mind to form an expression you're used to seeing, shake them loose. Choose fresh, specific language.

out with a specific verb, to make clear what "lay the foundations for" implies. The writer likely means prepare for, build, encourage, or instill.

Resist lifeless verbs and phrases. Think of what you are trying to say and write *that*, instead.

* * *

Freshness in your writing: the creative insight and originality that makes a meaningful impression on readers and stays with them. To achieve this, try experimenting with lively and accurate verbs.

Toni Morrison's novels, for example, are rhapsodies of verbs. Her language tantalizes the imagination, propelling memory, thought, and sensation with words so energized you feel them race through your body. Her words make you wonder, *Where is this awakening going to take me?* She established this dynamic with her first novel, *The Bluest Eye*, in which she describes june bugs shooting everywhere, black garters biting into brown stockings, faces "knotted like dark cauliflowers." As the child Claudia suffers a fever one night,

> . . . feet padded into the room, hands repinned the flannel, re-adjusted the quilt, and rested a moment on my forehead. So when I think of autumn, I think of somebody with hands who does not want me to die.

Such a moving portrait of love; simple and specific. This passage contrasts with the larger subject of *The Bluest Eye*—a different kind of love. Love without grace. Morrison confronts the spiritual harm and self-loathing that can destroy those who yearn to follow convention but don't fit the ideal. When marriage and housework leave a woman named Pauline depleted and alone, she soothes herself by going to the movies. But on a deep level, Hollywood's picture of perfection only adds to her distress. What Pauline absorbs about love and beauty, Morrison writes, "originated in envy, thrived in insecurity, and ended in disillusion. In equating physical beauty with virtue, she stripped her mind, bound it, and collected self-contempt by the heap."

This series of verb-driven images is sharp, brief, original. Morrison takes us into Pauline's psychological behaviors, describing them with visceral verbs that light scenes in my mind. The driving physicality of her language fires my imagination. I read "ended in disillusion" and for some reason I picture dead love like a great, thick robe, sliding off bare skin to the floor. The violence of "stripped" and "bound" snaps and stings. "Collected . . . by the heap" whips me back to the end of love and standing exposed and cold, with the thing that used to warm me now lying useless at my ankles. Pauline's bruising epiphany pulls me into her story.

Morrison, a virtuoso of rhythm as well as poetic imagery, creates a lasting effect with her active verbs. Her accents fall on the verbs; they strike like the tolling of a heavy bell.

* * *

You are in charge of your work. The realities of writing are too vast, complex, and nuanced for strict rules that dictate nevers, alwayses and don'ts. How readers enter your work, absorb it, and respond to it is—for the most part—up to you. (I qualify this because one can't possibly anticipate every misinterpretation; one could sooner please every star in the sky.)

This is why language choices are crucial.

And good reasons exist for choosing the passive voice.

Clouding things over to some degree makes sense, say, when you're focusing on certain facts rather than who is presenting them.

Naming the doers is not always necessary. And so we welcome the passive voice back onstage.

It's not wise to eliminate the passive voice in every case. Instead, use the passive voice with care and intention.

Sometimes it's smart to skip the doer. Sensitive schoolteachers, for example, can avoid pointing fingers with a kinder, face-saving suggestion:

> "Listen up! Lulu left her lunch box on her desk, and now it's gone. *Maybe it's been picked up accidentally.* What can we do about this?"

Using the passive voice removes the doer and emphasizes the receiver. In the italicized sentence above, that's the lunch box. The important thing is to find it, not assign blame.

In certain instances, skipping the doer with the passive voice is the most streamlined choice. For example, with complex matters, passive voice can convey facts in the simplest way. To do this, think about what's most necessary for readers to know. Reporting on the inquiry into George Floyd's death, Erin Donaghue of CBS News begins in active voice, then shifts to passive:

> George Floyd, the Minnesota man who *died* after an officer arresting him *pressed* his knee onto his neck, *died* by homicide, according to the results of two autopsies *released* on Monday—one by the county medical examiner and the other

> by independent pathologists *commissioned by* Floyd's family. [Italics are mine.]

After reporting the big news here—death by homicide—Donaghue calls attention to the source of the news, the autopsy results. Identifying who released the results comes later, and who commissioned one of the autopsies comes later still. This is appropriate because the results themselves are the main focus. Donaghue also writes in the passive voice when she mentions charges against one of the police officers involved:

> The Minneapolis officer *seen* kneeling on Floyd's neck, Derek Chauvin, *was charged* last week with third-degree murder and second-degree manslaughter. [Italics are mine.]

This spotlights *the person* receiving the state's charges in the killing. It's simple and clear. But if you swap in the active voice, you risk confusion. Active verbs take the focus off Chauvin, and because you have to name other groups of people, the sentence gets messy. Like this: Last week prosecutors charged Derek Chauvin, the Minneapolis officer whom witnesses and viewers of onlookers' videos saw kneeling on Floyd's neck, with third-degree murder and second-degree manslaughter.

No need to spell out who saw Chauvin kneeling or that prosecutors are the ones filing the charges. That's understood.

* * *

The passive voice is also appropriate in science or technical writing, pointing up experiments, findings, and facts, rather than the researchers who made and discovered them:

- Large and consistent decreases in April snowpack *have been observed* throughout the western United States.
- Although most of the valley's archeological sites *have been picked over* and many of the artifacts *removed*, important finds *are still* occasionally *reported.*

Still, writers of scientific, technical, and historical reports—and any other writers—should avoid piling on the passive voice. Instructional text, especially, will only grow dull, lifeless, and difficult to read. From an ornithological guide:

> With all eggs *received* in exchange or otherwise, this note *should*, if possible, *be obtained* in the handwriting of the person from whom they *are received*, and the slip on which it *is written be affixed* in the book under the number. When specimens of the eggs of the same species *are obtained* from various localities, those from each locality *should be distinguished* by a letter *prefixed to* the number. The plan *will be better understood* by referring to the following extract . . .

Alas, if that next extract is like this one, the plan stands little chance.

Compare these two passages:

> Version A: In 1933 the recreational potential of the canyon *was finally recognized* and land for the Palo Duro Canyon State Park *was purchased* by the State of Texas with money *obtained* through a public revenue bond issue. Today, most of the park revenue *received* through gate admissions, concession receipts, and mineral leases goes into a fund that pays off the remaining balance of the revenue bonds. [Passive voice in italics.]

> Version B: In 1933 the State of Texas finally *saw* the canyon's recreational potential and *issued* a public revenue bond *to buy* land for the Palo Duro Canyon State Park. Today, most of the park's revenue from gate admissions, concession receipts, and mineral leases pays off the remaining balance of the revenue bonds. [Verb changes in italics.]

The history brightens when you replace the passive voice with active-voice verbs. And when you substitute long verbs with short ones: *saw* instead of *recognized*, *buy* over *purchased*. The second version highlights doers and actions, and makes the ho-hum administrative process more direct and understandable. It's also shorter.

* * *

George Orwell's final rule in "Politics and the English Language" is to break his rules "sooner than say anything outright barbarous." Hear, hear. As I've mentioned above, it does no good to slash and burn the passive voice. First think about what you want to say, and how to make it clear. The key is to keep the picture you want to paint in mind, as vividly as possible, and experiment with precise, evocative verbs and their voice. Tinker and tune, word by word, phrase by phrase, to find the mix that brightens your scene and shapes the spirit and perspective you want.

We've looked at examples of smart use of passive-voice verbs in journalism and technical writing. Now let's turn to literature, and how with thoughtful use, the passive voice can convey just the right shade of meaning and a powerful effect.

James Joyce is an expert at controlling how readers approach his work. He uses the power of language choice to adjust the aperture so we see his images in a particular way. At the opening of *Ulysses*, he introduces us to Buck Mulligan in one of literature's greatest entrances:

> Stately, plump Buck Mulligan came from the stairhead, bearing a bowl of lather on which a mirror and a razor lay crossed. A yellow dressinggown, ungirdled, was sustained gently behind him by the mild morning air. He held the bowl aloft and intoned:
>
> —*Introibo ad altare Dei.*
>
> Halted, he peered down the dark winding stairs and called up coarsely:
>
> —Come up, Kinch. Come up, you fearful jesuit.

Of all the marvelous images in this opening, I'm drawn to that yellow gown floating on daylight. Joyce's use of the passive construction "was sustained" directs the mind's eye first to the shape and movement of the fabric, drifting like a wedding dress train, like a poetic extension of Mulligan himself. Or rather, like the self-image that Mulligan holds in his mind: the center of attention, otherworldly, his open gown in a standout color leaving a lasting impression on an imagined public watching him pass.

Joyce, with his astute passive voice, also manages to stress action. I read his description and wonder how one passes in such a way as to sustain a bubble of dressing gown. Having told us Buck Mulligan is stately, now Joyce shows us his particular manner of stateliness in a moving image full of mock-heroic sweep and drama. "Was sustained" emphasizes the gown and its central part in this performative entrance. Why write it this way? It presents a double perspective, Mulligan's and, at the same time, Joyce's. One is idealized, the other frank, mildly ridiculing, and possibly brutal.

Sherwood Anderson works the element of perspective in a different way in this passage from his short story "The Egg":

> In town he drank several glasses of beer and stood about in Ben Head's saloon. Songs were sung and glasses thumped on the bar.

Anderson, a master of the short-story form, begins with his protagonist doing things, all in the active voice. Then the author shifts to passive. Why? He's focusing on the blunt behaviors of a crowd, intensifying its physicality. In the short, one-syllable verbs we feel the reckless exuberance of barflies who've blurred into a faceless mass.

With "thumped," Anderson paints a portrait. Note that "glasses thumped" could be an active-voice construction in another instance. Here, though, Anderson implies that glasses *were thumped* on the bar (by the crowd), just as songs *were sung*. What a difference if he'd written "glasses were set forcefully on the bar" or some such clunker. In this instance, using passive voice doesn't rob the verbs of effect. It emphasizes the universality, suggesting a heaving throng, so indistinct and unified in purpose that it roars and clanks about as one.

Speaking of eggs: Cookbooks often feature lively imagery and verb use, and one of my favorite authors in this arena is Juliet Corson, a visionary cookery instructor of the late 1800s. In the example below, she breaks from the active voice to highlight the widespread manner of preparing a dish. For a basic scramble:

> Usually this omelette is served soft—as soft as ice cream.

She doesn't name the people doing the serving, which is "most cooks," because that's predictable and understood in context, and she is focused on the omelette. But if you wish to emphasize specific, out-of-the-ordinary cooks, name them and use the active voice, like this: Ridley's grandpa serves this omelette deep-fried—like funnel cake, in a quart of oil.

* * *

My point is to use active or passive voice with intent. The passive voice can be a trap if writers lean on it unwisely. It's easier to slide into the passive voice when faced with a deadline or a topic about which we're not terribly confident. The passive voice can lure writers into imitating grandee-speak or the thick academic style of specialists and scholars—and trust me, in my very long career I have made these mistakes before. That kind of flab doesn't equal sophistication; it's only vague and confusing.

But remember that the range of effects with verbs is wide, whether the verbs are active or passive. The passive voice can present facts efficiently. In many instances, it can be a strong stylistic choice.

Use the passive voice with discretion, to enhance your prose without cluttering it. The secret lies in care and intention.

* * *

Good Habits

Find a brief news article and highlight each verb in it. How many are in active voice, and how many in passive voice? Rewrite the passive-voice sentences in active voice. This may improve some but not others. Why is that?

Choose a paragraph from a book and rewrite it, switching what passive-voice constructions you can to active voice. How does this change the text?

Try this with several paragraphs of your own writing. You can also revisit the text you used at the end of chapter 1. Rewrite any passive-voice constructions in active voice. Does this shorten your sentences? Compare with your original version. Has your meaning become clearer? Or does using the active voice make the sentences more confusing? Now put yourself in your reader's position. Is the account easy to grasp, does it flow and feel natural? Play around with passive and active voice until you find a mix that pleases you.

CHAPTER 4

Sharpen

Keys to masterful adverbs—and avoiding them with the right verb.

I am dead to adverbs; they cannot excite me.

—MARK TWAIN

Adverbs: slipping irresistibly in place, with their rhythmic *-ly*—softly, soothingly, seductively—and their promises of richness, their siren song of necessity.

Inessential adverbs: resistible. Left unchecked, they're like a sticky little invasive species.

In this chapter, we'll explore the perils of adverbs, when they're just plain wrong or redundant, how to avoid the pitfalls, and how to let them shine.

Adverbs, which describe, qualify, or limit verbs as well as adjectives and other adverbs, are often unnecessary. Avoid those that repeat or exaggerate an idea. For example:

> In fact, she realized, he hadn't said a word directly to her since she'd thrown herself briefly into his arms. Paradoxically, the quality of his silence was saying a lot of things rather loudly,

and all of them were making Alexandra's heart stutter like a stone skipped across a lake.

We can gather that the silent seducer in this steamy romp is a raging inferno inside, and Alexandra is smitten. (What a lovely stone-skipping image.) Five adverbs accompany her revelation: *directly*, *briefly*, *paradoxically*, *rather*, and *loudly*. Do they add or detract? Is saying a word directly to someone distinct from saying a word *to* someone?

Sometimes a single, excellent adverb can add just the right touch of insight, intensity, and brilliance. To achieve this, choose adverbs with care, in service to writing that is clear and meaningful.

We all use adverbs, and overuse them, so much that they become reflexive and meaning*less*. In small doses, we hardly notice them. (Okay, you caught me.) But like barnacles, they can cluster around verbs, modifying them in many ways, not all of them good. They label more than describe. They can sap energy, wreck efficiency, and impede flow.

Opt for restraint, or adverbs will drag down your writing.

The good news is that adverbs are often expendable, and avoiding overuse is easy. How? By choosing the right verb.

Adverbs tell us how, where, how often, when, and to what extent an action is performed. Words such as *here*, *never*, and *yesterday*, for example, are adverbs that specify where, how often, and when. These can be essential to meaning: You'll have to wait here. Lunch never begins before noon. The Federation announced the ban yesterday. (Note that some adverbs can also be adjectives or nouns: I'd like to adopt this dog here. She's looking for yesterday's mail.)

The problem lies with adverbs of manner (how an action is performed) or emphasis (to what extent). Words such as *smoothly*, *rudely*, *absolutely*, etc. can fluff up a basic, beige multipurpose verb, adding details to achieve the sense a writer wants. But instead of tacking an adverb onto a boring verb, choose a vivid, dynamic verb to convey the same thought on its own *without* an adverb.

Choose a precise verb that makes adverbs unnecessary.

Compare these two sentences:

Version A: Making his way awkwardly into the spa on crutches, he called out loudly to the pedicurist that she's the reason he got into an accident and he's suing her for going wildly over the top with the foot lotion.

Version B: Hobbling into the spa on crutches, he hollered at the pedicurist that she's the reason he wrecked his Ferrari and he's suing her for slathering.

"Making his way" and "got into" are basic, boring verbs that can be replaced with more dynamic ones. "Called out" implies loudness, and "going over the top" implies wildness. Trim away bloat and redundancies with sharp verbs. Version B is shorter, smoother, and has some bite.

Long, multisyllabic words take more time to speak, and they also take more time to read—and more time for the reader to process. They clog the flow. Adverbs with *-ly* endings are prone to clogging, because they stretch at least to two syllables, often more. *Unsurprisingly, bewilderingly, lackadaisically*: What clunkers!

Worst of all, they can waste the reader's time.

"Sorry I snitched on you," he said apologetically.

"You're still going to die," she replied menacingly.

Do we need to know an apology was apologetic? Cut the adverbs and you strengthen both sentences.

Avoid adverbs in sentences containing obvious meanings.

Better to trust the reader and let the characters talk, let them fall into a rhythm. When you're attributing dialogue—*if* you even need to say who's talking—the simplest unadorned verb is best. As Stephen King put it, "While to write adverbs is human, to write 'he said' or 'she said' is divine." What he means is that "he said" and "she said" don't distract the reader. They disappear—a divine trick, indeed. They melt into the page so that readers scan right over "said" and focus instead on *what* was said.

If someone speaks in an unexpected way while threatening murder, express that with an apt verb:

"You're still going to die," she whispered.

* * *

If adverbs are so often superfluous, why do so many writers use them? We're used to them. Rhythm is an important quality in speech and writing, and adverbs can add a conventional drumbeat:

Justin Bieber and Selena Gomez ~~basically~~ poured their relationship into their songs.

> Selena's "Love Will Remember" ~~literally~~ contains a voicemail from Justin.

Actually, basically, crucially, honestly, literally, seriously, surprisingly, and, least interesting of all, *interestingly*: Grammarians call these adverbs of emphasis. They are also crutch words, because it's common to lean on these adverbs like a crutch, to prop up sentences that might seem weak without them.

> "Try the bourbon-glazed donut burger," said Scratch. "It's literally blowing my mind!"

Yet Scratch's mind, despite the sugar high, remains intact. He's embellishing and exaggerating—the opposite of "literally," which means keeping to the facts.

Why weigh down the verb phrase "blowing my mind," weakening it with the misunderstood adverb "literally"? Like many adverbs, crutch words aren't necessary. They can even contradict the verbs they modify. We all use them—they surely lurk in these pages—and they won't kill anyone. But most of the time they don't add anything meaningful.

Adverbial crutches are everywhere and misused in the extreme. *Actually* is one of the most annoying and overused words in the English language. It doesn't have to be that way. Its correct use emphasizes something real (the actual) in contrast with the theoretical or imagined:

> I thought we were just meeting for drinks, which is why I offered to pay. Actually, Blair ordered a ton of food and the bill was obscene.

Clear enough. But perhaps you've felt that flash of oh-no-here-it-comes when someone seeks to rope you into their overthinking drama and they "actually" you, using the adverb to twist reality for personal gain or to avoid responsibility:

> I'm getting blamed for the food poisoning, but AC-SHU-A-LY you all ate my clam dip on your own so it's not my fault. Did I force you?

When he was vice president, Joe Biden peppered a speech with adverbial crutches at the Democratic National Convention. *Politico* reported that he used *literally* nine times. Each use was incorrect. For example: "I want to show you the character of a leader who had what it took when the American people literally stood on the brink of a new depression."

People literally stood where? One cannot stand inside a metaphor. One can, however, put crutches to good use. As #literally raced through Twitter, the drinking games began.

* * *

Show, don't tell. It's the golden rule, a prized technique of narrative writing, playwriting, any writing.

Anton Chekhov noted that instead of stating it's a moonlit night, it's better to write that "on the mill dam a piece of glass from a broken bottle glittered like a bright little star, and that the black shadow of a dog or a wolf rolled past like a ball."

Glittered. Rolled past. Chekhov's vivid, dynamic verbs energize this passage. They fuel the poetic and specific details that show moonlight in action, and what the scene looks and feels like.

"Cross out as many adjectives and adverbs as you can," he wrote.

Adverbs tend to steer the unwary writer toward telling, as opposed to showing with an effective description, which can be more expressive and meaningful to the reader.

Here is a sentence that tells instead of shows: "When La Bellabooma hit the high C, the crowd *loudly cheered*."

First, the obvious: When a crowd cheers, it's loud; no need for the adverb. Second, the statement is dull. More fun to show the effects of those mighty lungs, with a vivid verb, an image, words that make the reader's heart swell and lift in sympathy.

Did the crowd roar as if Juan Soto had barreled a ball past the orchestra and beyond the balcony? Did it sound like the BeyHive in force when Beyoncé commands a stadium?

And amid the noise, did a tear slip down the cheek of an operagoer on the aisle, the sign, perhaps, of some long-buried ache that the diva's voice set free?

* * *

I face show-don't-tell situations with every feature story and review I write. Here's one that stands out: A few years ago, the New York City Ballet agreed to let me watch a young choreographer named Justin Peck create a dance for the company's upcoming season. My heart leaped. Artists at work don't often throw open the door to a reporter—let alone a critic. And Peck, age twenty-six at the time, was a rising star. (He's now soaring; as of this book's publication, he's won three Tonys.)

But how would I make the most of this moment? One option: Sit through the rehearsal with the goal of outlining it in a few words, then meet with Peck afterward and ask him to tell me about the high points and explain his creative process. But that approach wouldn't immerse readers in the bouncy exuberance of Peck's work, or show them what fresh creativity feels like. I wanted to bring readers with me, let them see what I saw, hear what I heard, feel what I felt. I relish the drama of a dance rehearsal, where everyone's puzzling out how these huge turning gears of people and patterns fit together. Any minute the whole production can seize up. Steps or timing or imagination can go awry. And yet you might glimpse inspiration itself: The choreographer comes up with a fix on the fly, or a dancer experiences a breakthrough. The intricate *work* of ballet-making is fascinating, unlike any other process. All this, I was certain, would make a strong story.

When I arrived, however, my plan to cast light on this secret laboratory seemed far-fetched. The rehearsal looked like chaos. Or a circus, ruled by a giant hive mind.

I gave myself time to absorb the frenetics, then fixed my attention on discrete actions, catching the look, sound, and feel of the scene bit by bit. I scribbled little details and the most vigorous verbs that flew to mind. It turned into great fun, and a good story. (It also, by luck, foretold a major success; with this ballet, titled *Everywhere We Go*, Peck shot to fame.) Here's an excerpt:

> The pianist races along with terrific propulsion; the music is all galloping drive and slippery swoops. Trying to keep up, two dancers bump into each other; another one stumbles and is nearly steamrolled by the next wave of flying legs.
>
> Peck, sporting a few days' razor stubble, looks Mardi Gras–eccentric in a bicycle-print T-shirt and striped coverall folded at his waist so the shoulder straps dangle and flap as he rockets around. He sings out the beat, pokes at his glasses, tries to back up and bumps into the mirror.
>
> "Don't jump!" he tells the dancers. Then, "Jump like popcorn!" And, casually, he orders the impossible: "Don't leave your feet on the floor too long."
>
> At times he is not at all sure how to get past the count of five. "Can I have, uh …" He stops, mouth open, a finger in the

air. Little eternities tick by. Dust settles, continents drift, the universe expands. Global warming? The crisis here is the dancers' muscles, cooling.

"Sorry," Peck says finally. "I just went to a different world there. Can you guys . . ." Another open-mouthed pause. Everyone waits. Lacking the words, Peck demonstrates; his lanky body knows what he wants. He whips around, stops, changes direction. The others copy him.

He pulls up the neck of his T-shirt and chews it thoughtfully.

"Harrison," he says. "You're going the wrong way."

And: "That's weird. I thought I told you guys to go *that* way."

"Those were terrible lines! But we'll fix them later."

Two hours go by.

"I am going to drink *so much* vodka tonight," murmurs one dancer to another with an extravagant eye roll.

Action, verb-driven images, colorful quotes (which are a form of action)—I was hoping these would show readers what it all felt like. I wanted Peck's voice and his character to come through in the quotes. And the ballerina's boozy remark: so witty and real! I included it to add surprise and perspective, and to emphasize her exhaustion.

But for all the action, I count four adverbs: *nearly*, *casually*, *finally*, and *thoughtfully*. Any more and I'd have dragged down the pace, when I wanted vigor and dash.

This is why I urge you to approach adverbs with caution. A large part of using verbs to improve your writing is clearing away redundancies and wasted words so the actions can shine. Choosing adverbs well, if at all, is part of the clearing-away process.

All too often, adverbial phrases weigh down the verb—phrases like "softly creep," "quickly scurry." They can also gum up your grammar. Among the worst offenders:

- **Join together.**

  Stand together, sit together, get your life and sh*t together. But unless you are singing along with The Who, you need not join together.

  Join is enough. It contains multitudes. *Join* is not so inadequate that it needs bucking up with adverbs.

  Webster's New World College Dictionary on *join*: "to put or bring *together*."

Join me in saluting clear and lucid eloquence. Let us also pledge, with or without a *Webster's* at hand, to respect the reader's time and good sense, and to respect our own. We vow also to take care of our writing, to promote excellence, and to do all of this by avoiding erroneous, unnecessary adverbs and adverbial phrases like these:

- **Feel badly.**

  Do you feel sadly when you read that? Neither do I, but I do feel bad. *Feel* is what's known as a linking verb. (See chapter 2 for more on these.) Common linking verbs are those of *being*: *be*, *become*, *seem*—and verbs of *sensing*: *feel*, *smell*, *look*, *taste*, *sound*. These verbs don't describe action; instead, they define their subject, as in: That house is a money pit. The verb links the subject with a complement, a word or phrase that defines it or gives an impression. A linking verb is like an equal sign: He seems kind. (He = kind.) The kitchen looks clean. (Kitchen = clean.)

Kind, *clean*: These are adjectives. They have to be, because they describe the subject of the sentence—a noun. Which brings me to why *badly*, an adverb, is incorrect with the linking verb *feel*. For example:

"Markie feels bad about the accident": *bad* is an adjective telling us about Markie. This sentence is correct.

"Markie feels badly about the accident" is not.

Swap *feel* with any other linking verb and you'll see why adverbs don't work.

"That cough sounds serious" is correct.

"That cough sounds seriously" makes no sense.

"Fido smells funky"—yes; grab the hose.

"Fido smells funkily"—nope. Unless Fido has an unusual upper respiratory system, in which case *smells* is not a linking verb but a standard action verb, describing Fido's ability to perceive scent. (Verbs: So versatile! No end to their marvels.)

Feeling curious about the rest? Here are more adverbial phrases to avoid.

- **Summarize briefly.**

  To summarize is *literally* to put in brief form. (Now please dismiss *literally* from your mind. Thank you.)

- **Whisper softly.**

  One can only whisper that way.

- **Quietly release.**

  Banish this from press releases and headlines. No doubt you have seen such breathless reports as "Syd's Superstore Quietly Released Deals Ahead of Its Huge Spring Sale" or "Console King Just Quietly Released the Game of the Decade." In most cases deals and products arrive with an unquiet flurry of marketing. PR departments do not seek attention quietly. They blast editors with ad campaigns.

- **Completely eliminate.**

  One cannot eliminate in degrees nor eliminate halfway or in portions. One eliminates and is done with it. No questions, no evidence, no adverb.

- **Completely destroy.**

- **Completely thwart.**

- **Completely rend my poor, nerdy heart.**

  Destroy, *thwart*, and *rend* get the job done all by themselves.

- **Gently simmer.**

  I'll admit that I have, on one or more occasions, dialed past simmer to boil and ended up with burnt rice and a pot to match. I've overlooked the little bubbles frothing to the surface, signifying the perfect, mellow temperature that would have gentled my basmati and saved my pot. Gentleness, I've learned the hard way, is an essential characteristic of the verb *simmer*.

- **Carefully examine.**

  As the *Webster's New World* at my elbow puts it, *examine* means "to look at or into critically or methodically in order to find out the facts, condition, etc., of; investigate; inspect; scrutinize; inquire into." I want my doctor to examine my X-rays, not glance at, skim, or scan them. *Carefully* should be baked into the bill.

- **Postpone until later.**

  Here on Earth we're stuck with the forward march of time. Postponing until *earlier* (preponing?) happens in that other universe, the one where I did not toss my mother's cashmere sweater—radical shade of orange, little zipper up the back—into the dryer.

- **Preplan/Forward plan.**

  To plan is to arrange or decide in advance. Planning precedes; it anticipates the future, it happens before. The meaning of this complete and perfect verb needs no reinforcing.

- **Concentrate intently.**

  Concentrate has a few meanings, but they all concern increasing direction, strength, or intensity, in one's attention or in frozen orange juice or what have you. In other words, for mental focus, concentrating is eleven. You can't dial it higher.

- **Diligently persist.**

  Persistence is all. Keep going, believe in your abilities, never give up, and never use an adverb that repeats the meaning of the verb.

- **Loudly roar/shout/yell.**

  You get the idea.

- **Quickly hop/jump/run.**

  These actions can only be done quickly, unless you're in that other place, the one with fresh, bouncy vintage cashmere that fits me.

  Leaping, however, can be quick *or* sustained. This is the dancer's art, to turn discipline into wonders, as a writer does by finding just the right verb, or, when necessary, adverb.

Avoid "there is."

Which sentence do you find more powerful?

> Nothing is more disagreeable than a piece of fish half raw at the bone.

> There is nothing more disagreeable than a piece of fish half raw at the bone.

Juliet Corson, the cookery teacher and author, wrote the first. She took an efficient, businesslike approach to devising nutritious meals for the poor, and she disliked waste in cooking—and writing.

The adverb *there* is unnecessary in most cases. We use it by habit but it's overkill. It shows that something exists ("There exists nothing more disagreeable . . ."), but why slap on a sticky note if you've already used a highlighter? In the following examples, dropping *there* from Option A strengthens Option B:

A. There will be hours of time spent there by children and daycare workers.
B. Children and daycare workers will spend hours there.

A. There were all sorts of testimonials from sports photographers and columnists about the difficulty of synchronized swimming.
B. Sports photographers and columnists gushed over the difficulty of synchronized swimming.

Used with care, adverbs can transform a sentence by adding depth and intensity that a verb alone can't. How do we recognize the masterful use of an adverb? When it intensifies a feeling in an efficient but rich and surprising way. When that one well-chosen word delivers additional information with an unexpected charge.

The secret to an essential adverb is specificity. Each word, adverb or not, should enhance your writing and add to its coherence, not overwhelm it.

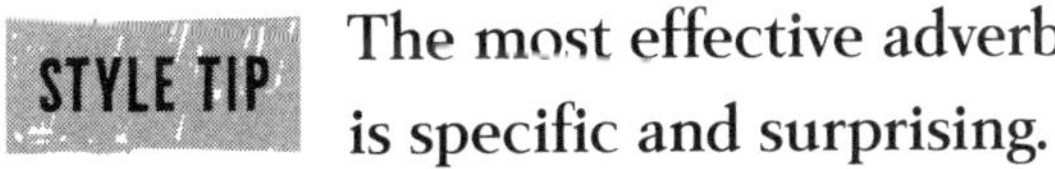

Adverbs, as we've seen, can become needless props. But take a look at this passage by John Dos Passos, from *Manhattan Transfer*. Dos Passos turns a barbershop experience into a study of choking helplessness, and every image underscores that feeling:

> When the barber threw back the chair to shave him he wanted to crane his neck like a mudturtle turned over on its back. The lather spread drowsily on his face, prickling his nose, filling up his ears.

His first sentence combines vivid verbs and participles with a mudturtle metaphor that delivers the instant sensation of awkwardness and entrapment. Following this, the adverb *drowsily* leaps out, dramatizing the action of a consequential noun—the lather—in an unexpected and specific way. Alone, *spread* is unspecific and bland. But with the adverb, Dos Passos heightens the tension. He gives the spreading lather a slow, careless quality, almost a will of its own, indifferent to the man beneath it. We picture and *feel* its blithe incursion on the orifices of this unnerved, disoriented fellow. We can make our own imaginative leaps as to how it invades and mutes his senses. Without *drowsily* the sentence loses the measure of time and an aspect of captivity.

A single adverb—not a string of them, but a lone, perfect pearl—can magnify the intensity of a simple statement. In her novel *Swing Time*, Zadie Smith describes a hot day in an unspecified West African country, where locals and officials spend hours in the sun, waiting for a self-absorbed pop star to kick off the opening of a school. To emphasize the scene's preposterousness, Smith directs us to this grouping:

> A troop of young soldiers dressed in dark blue uniforms stood in the middle, holding their brass instruments, brutally sweating.

Brutally is a surprising way to describe something as normal and involuntary as sweating, but how right it is here. How *palpable*. It intensifies *sweating*, and drives us inside those uniforms, the fabric drenched, the body swelling and suffering. The word carries overtones of the military itself: hardness, enforcement. It's the kind of word soldiers would use. They're not going to say, for instance, "I'm wilting." And however brutal the sweating, it is not causing them to wilt. The soldiers are bearing up and we see that, too, as they stand with their trumpets. Smith's adverb is unusual and figurative yet it suits her subject and intensifies the emotion. Unusual, perfect, and not at all showy, it also underscores the author's offhand grace.

Juxtapose adverb and verb. An unexpected pairing boosts emotion and intensifies your meaning.

Juxtapositions in writing get our attention. Combine an aggressive adverb (*brutally*) with a tame contrasting action and the action intensifies. The clash is the gin and the tonic, the sauna and the snow. A sharp juxtaposition deepens our understanding, rather than underscoring what we already know. This is another secret of effective adverb use.

Notice how the authors I've just mentioned—Dos Passos and Smith—use the technique of juxtaposing.

Here's another, from the landmark 1857 French novel *Madame Bovary*. Author Gustave Flaubert rose to fame for the stylistic beauty and realism of his unsparing (and, at the time, shocking) story of adultery. You see both beauty and realism in the passage below, a meeting between Emma Bovary and one of her lovers. Note that Flaubert pairs *brutally* with the basic verb *undress*:

> Emma returned to him more avid, more breathless and enflamed than ever before. She undressed brutally, ripping off

> the thin laces of her corset so violently that they would whistle round her hips like a gliding snake.

Beat by beat, Flaubert ramps up his heroine's emotional state until he shows us her frenzy in specific actions. The picture of sexual abandon is so clear that, in a famous obscenity trial against Flaubert, France's imperial counsel quoted this passage. Even the lawyer, though, was moved to describe it as "an admirable painting with respect to talent."

What I'm talking about here is calibration. Measure your chosen verb against the intention and feeling that you want. Does it generate the desired tone? Leave it alone.

Can the sparing use of a perfect adverb sharpen it, add personality, or take your reader further into the heart of the moment? Let your intuition and creativity lead the way.

* * *

Good Habits

Here's an exercise in showing, not telling. Remember that showing lets readers experience your story for themselves, through emotions and the senses. Telling, by contrast, outlines an event with few sensory details. Take a look at this excerpt from a brief history of nineteenth-century celebrity Fanny Elssler, an Austrian ballerina:

> Less than two weeks after landing in New York she assembled the best dancers she could and made her debut on May 14. The audience went wild and the Park Theatre was sold out for her entire stay. No matter what she danced or how well, the ovation was the same.

Plunge into these events in a short descriptive scene or two, 250 words or so. What drama erupts as Fanny assembles artists she's never met before? How can you *show* that the audience went wild? What did the ovation sound and feel like? Use your imagination and vivid verbs.

Here are more prompts. Write brief, immersive, verb-filled scenes to show what happens and drench readers in emotion. (Pour it on first, edit later.)

1. A friend arrives at your home with her dog. Yours streaks out the door, the friend's dog follows, neighbors join you in chasing them—and you realize you're all headed straight for a fancy outdoor wedding.
2. As you're leaving the dry cleaner's one wintry day with shirts in one hand, tote in the other, you slip on the ice and slam to the ground. Phone, laptop, clothes, and keys skid across the parking lot toward the dumpster just as the trash truck rumbles in.
3. While biking to work one morning, you round a corner and surprise a couple of bear cubs pawing through a trash can they've knocked into the street. You hop off your bike to avoid plowing into them. Mama bear, sunning herself in a nearby driveway, jumps to her feet.

When you've finished writing, highlight any adverbs. Can you cut them without losing meaning? Will a clearer verb help? Check a thesaurus for alternatives to a basic verb that has just the shade of meaning you want. I'm partial to the classic *Roget's Thesaurus of English Words and Phrases* and my thumb-indexed *New American Roget's College Thesaurus in Dictionary Form.* Also good: *Actions: The Actors' Thesaurus* by Marina

Caldarone and Maggie Lloyd-Williams and the online thesauruses at merriam-webster.com and onelook.com.

Try the exercise above with other brief, intense experiences you've had; describe them with verbs to show what they *felt* like.

CHAPTER 5

Weed

From blah to brilliant: Methods for sending snoozy *be* verbs (and others) to their eternal rest. Pointers for replacing such verbal vexations as the pretentious, the jargony, and the boring.

Hear the links fall in place
And the sturdy padlock clinking

—ELIZABETH JENNINGS, "VERB"

As I write this book, I hear the voice of Mrs. Culhane in my head. She was my fourth-grade teacher, a tall, elegant woman with white hair swirling in a perfect pouf. She dressed for business—wool skirt suits, sparkly brooches—and she got down to it.

Did she care that we were nine? Not at all. In Mrs. Culhane's class I read *Madame Curie* (her choice) and *Madame Bovary* (mine; I was bored by the romance, intrigued by the ruin). Mrs. Culhane had a way of boiling down the mysteries of writing to their bones so you could see how they fit together.

Each Monday, for instance, she wrote an overused word or phrase on an index card and entombed it in the Word Graveyard, a tidy set of paper pockets that hung on the wall. Bland verbs landed there often, which meant we couldn't use them in our writing for the rest of the week.

One week she killed off *to be*—gold stars if we swapped smart synonyms for any of its forms. Another week: *to do*. RIP *is* and *was*, *did* and *done*. Hello, lively choices! Mrs. Culhane encouraged us to expand our vocabulary and find new ways to describe things, especially actions. ~~This was life changing.~~ This changed my life. I ~~am~~ remain forever grateful, for the Word Graveyard pushed me to improve my writing with the boundless expressive power of verbs.

STYLE TIP Replace *be* verbs with verbs of action.

"I always wanted to be someone," said comedian Lily Tomlin. "Now I realize I should have been more specific."

She's right. You've noticed, no doubt, a strong preference here for verbs of *doing*. Verbs of being—*be*, and also *become*, *appear*, *seem*—have their place, but efficient, specific action verbs give readers more detail. Imagine an ambitious person replacing her vague wish "to be someone" with concrete desires: to conquer comedy, halt famine, or explode physics with theories of, oh, I don't know, post-quantum gravity. Who knows when great quests may take shape? Dream in action-verb infinitives, young friend! You may reach your goal faster. In any form, *be* verbs often add length and slow the pace. When you write, try replacing them with a more definite verb tense, or with another verb altogether.

Compare these sentences:

> The staff *was playing Candy Crush* while the candidate *was droning on* about taxes.

> The staff *played Candy Crush* while the candidate *droned on* about taxes.

The first sentence contains the imperfective aspect (featured in chapter 2) of the verbs *play* and *droned on*. The second one speeds by with the sharp, definite past tense.

Many options exist for replacing a *be* verb, as you can see in these examples:

Ellery *is feeling like an idiot* for buying that fixer-upper.

Version A: Ellery *kicked himself* for buying that fixer-upper.

Version B: Ellery *broke out in hives and lived on gin for a week* after buying that fixer-upper.

Version A replaces a familiar, wordy phrase—"is feeling like an idiot"—with a strong reflexive verb.

Version B replaces the *be*-verb cliché with phrasal verbs and specific (if hyperbolic) details that *show* his feelings instead of simply *telling* readers how he felt.

* * *

However, verbs of being are appropriate when you want to describe the subject of the sentence by linking it to something else:

The story of *The Giver* by Lois Lowry *appears simple* but in fact *is not simple* at all. (Story = simple; story ≠ simple.)

Compare these:

A: You got rid of that cruet set? But it was a gift from your mother! (It = gift)

B: You got rid of that cruet set? But your mother gave it to you!

The difference is a matter of emphasis. Version A links the set with *gift*. It hints at what sacrifices and intentions might have gone into it. Version B stresses *mother* and the act of giving but lacks the emotional overtone of *gift*.

One bright, right verb can clear away clutter and make your sentence shine.

* * *

Think of the Word Graveyard, burial place for dull, tired verbs. Let's look at ways to improve your sentences with dynamic verbs that replace dull verbs, clunky verb phrases, and adverbs.

Replace *go*:

A. We went down the hill at a quick pace. (Weak, wordy.)
B. We descended quickly. (Still stodgy. Find a verb that describes speed and lose the adverb.)
C. We ran/rushed/flew down the hill. (Quick, clean, punchy.)

Replace *do*:

A. They may try, but they can't possibly ever do it. (Tedious—plus an unnecessary adverb.)
B. They may try, but they can't succeed. (What single verb means "unable to succeed"?)
C. They may try but they'll fail. (Simple and direct.)

Replace *have*:

A. He had a bunch of cash wadded up in his pockets.
B. He carried cash wadded up in his pockets.
C. His pockets bulged with cash.

Sometimes the less said, the better:

A. "I have no intention of accepting your offer," she declared. "It's crazy."
B. "I refuse to accept your crazy offer," she said.

Or skip the quote and inject a power move:

C. She laughed at him and left.

* * *

Do not confuse effective verbs with fancy verbs.

Remember that the guiding qualities of good writing are clarity and grace. Using verbs effectively can enhance these qualities and improve your writing, provided you do not confuse effective with fancy.

The best verb is often the simplest verb. No one sounds smarter or clearer by saying "utilize" rather than "use." They sound boring. Fancy verbs are pretentious, and unless that's the effect you're going for, they can interrupt the pleasing flow of your work.

I like to keep Stephen King's advice in mind: "To write 'he said' or 'she said' is divine." When I brought it up in chapter 4, my focus was on avoiding unnecessary adverbs. To build on that, here I'm calling attention to the good, clean plainness of the verb *say.* If you're attributing words to a speaker, opt for *say* or *said*—"You're under arrest," said the officer—and move on with your story. The reader wants to hear the dialogue, not what fancy verbs the writer throws in to whomp up the attribution. When writing dialogue or adding quotes in a news story or work of fiction, avoid such showy, fancy verbs as *commented, declared, pronounced, put in,* and *remarked.*

It's better to repeat a word than to make a show of not repeating it.

Don't worry about repeating *said* (or *asked*) throughout a conversation, even if you had a teacher who told you not to repeat words in a sentence, paragraph, or page.

Take a look at these examples from a romance novel:

> "Because you didn't want to live as a ruined spinster in Torquay?" he bit out.

You can bite out a short, sharp curse but not an elaborate put-down like that quote, especially when it's a question.

> "You've let the spurious claims of a sweet-faced female blind you to the facts," he ground out.

"Ground out" has a sense of brutal, mechanical action, which doesn't square with this character's flowery reproach.

Perhaps the author found "ground out" after a quick thesaurus search. A thesaurus is a treasure—I urge you to keep one or even a stack of them at hand and bookmark reliable websites (see my recommendations in the Good Habits section of chapter 4)—but a writer can't grab from a thesaurus in haste without considering whether the synonym is truthful. Synonyms and related words have shades of nuance that matter to one's meaning, and an ill-chosen verb can skew it. In effective writing, the verbs fit in a coherent way. They slide into place without friction.

* * *

Write to shed light in a fresh, direct way.

Do that by avoiding fancy verbs, unless you're spoofing some pompous character or you plan a witty, ironic twist. Fancy verbs are easy to spot; they often stretch to several syllables. Replace them with clear, simple verbs. Examples of fancy verbs:

Ameliorate. Improve it with *improve.*

Conceptualize. This is a word turducken—a verb (*conceive*) stuffed in a noun (*concept*) further wedged into a bloated, boring verb. I railed against *conceptualization* in chapter 2. Where will it all end—*conceptualizationize*? Better: *imagine*, *picture*, or *see.*

Elucidate. *Explain* says it all in half the syllables.

Emblazon. *Blazon*, without the *em-*, is wonderful on its own.

Entitle. As with *blazon*, adding an extra syllable—*en*—is unnecessary. *Title* suffices for the verb meaning to provide a title for, such as a book or movie. Use *entitle* to mean to give a legal right or claim to receive or do something.

Importune. *Beg* or *implore*—yes. *Importune* if you find yourself dining with Lord Byron and he's pushing his preference for vinegar and water upon you.

Opine. No one does this. People *say*, or, if they must, they *state*, *argue*, *insist*...

Utilize. Three syllables and all their attendant oxygen and time, instead of the simple, direct *use*—why on earth?

* * *

While we're on the subject of awkward verbs and ineffective usage, what do you make of this statement?

> "This is a really good business that we overshot on expense. And so we're trying to right-size that to make sure we can plant the seeds and make the investments in the things that we need."

The interim CEO of *The Washington Post* produced this babble at a company-wide meeting where she announced the largest staff reduction in years.

Overshoot, undershoot, overreach, right-size, drill down, do more with less, plant the seeds: Business jargon borrows from sports, construction, and farming to lend itself brawniness and vigor. But what does "plant the seeds" mean for employees who want to know if they'll still have a job?

Of course, my former employer isn't alone in relying on corporate-speak to soften the picture. Euphemisms veil bad news so executives can avoid saying it straight. It's "jargon monoxide," as Stanford management professor Robert Sutton told *Fortune* magazine. The magazine called out such vague terms as "right-sized," "simplified operating model," "corporate outplacing," and "org changes," which various tech and finance companies have used to announce job cuts.

In a broader sense, the real trouble is that people hear and read this doublespeak so often, they do not question it or fix it. The expressions are silly but some must see them as kind of cool, because well-intentioned people end up adopting them and releasing them into the wild. As a result, in everyday settings as well as in the office we hear folks talk in puffy generalities: pivoting, teeing up, giving 110 percent, moving the needle, next-leveling. The result is we don't know what they mean with any specificity. They may not either.

Nobody should use these clichés. Clear, strong, graceful writing chases vagueness and abstraction off the page, replacing them with details and genuine meaning.

* * *

Let's look at this chapter's epigraph, from Elizabeth Jennings's poem "Verb," the first section of her ode "Parts of Speech":

> Hear the links fall in place / And the sturdy padlock clinking

The lines capture the essential function of the verb: to secure the meaning of the sentence. Verbs express your meaning. The right verb is precise, honest, efficient. It clicks like a lock.

It does not distract with an ill fit.

Finding the best verb can take time. I know this well. Near the beginning of chapter 1, I wrote, "I have relied on the power of verbs every day of my career." Simple enough, but my sentence didn't start out that way. First I'd typed "I have leveraged the power of verbs . . . ," etc. Yuck, I thought later, reading it over. *Leverage*? Fancy verb alert!

I started scribbling options in a notebook, which is why I can take you through this process. *Summoned* sounded like I was invoking spirits; too much drama. Then *every* verb I tried—*invoked, called on, believed in*—brought crystal balls to mind. *Drawn on* felt la-di-da. *Depended on*? That states the obvious; every sentence depends on a verb. It's also a heavy word, a bit thunky. What a relief when *relied on* slid into place. *Merriam-Webster* defines *rely on* as "to need (someone or something) for support, help, etc.: to depend on (someone or something)," and that's what I meant. I have needed the right verbs to support what I was writing, particularly when writing about dance, and for my work to make sense and succeed.

I raise this example not to alarm you with weird obsessiveness—I don't go through this with every sentence—but to show you that to make your meaning clear, you often must rethink and rewrite. And always edit.

A perfect verb is specific to your objective and enlivens your sentence.

* * *

Good Habits

- Cultivate a healthy intolerance for insider-speak and fuzzy gibberish that passes for meaningful language. Read news articles and press releases for jargon. Rewrite those passages in simple, straightforward words.
- Scan everything you read for fancy verbs that sound pretentious to you. Make your own list of verbs and expressions to avoid.
- Find cases of "there is" in a piece of writing and rearrange those sentences. Evaluate the result. Are there instances where "there is" simply sounds better (as in this question)? Look for this construction in whatever you read, and notice when "there is" produces a welcome colloquial tone, or when it clutters.

PART II

THE POETIC

CHAPTER 6

Tantalize

Let the body talk: Physical action reveals the feels. Suggest the ineffable through your characters' behavior.

He had kicked himself loose of the earth.

—JOSEPH CONRAD, *HEART OF DARKNESS*

Verbs are intangible, inanimate, made of air and opinion. Changeable as they are, they play a major role in sparking feelings in the reader. Take advantage of their interpretive quality. An imaginative, surprising verb can snap an everyday action into starlight. A vigorous verb can kick off a witty metaphor. A snip of movement, caught with a clear, crisp verb, can pierce the heart. In these ways and more, verbs help light up the small, hot, hidden things we feel but can't always express. That's what we'll focus on at this point: the poetic power of verbs.

In this chapter we'll explore how evocative verbs can summon those teasing wisps of mystery that make up suggestion. Harness the power of verbs and you can imply thoughts and emotions, while letting readers come to their own conclusions.

Suggestion intrigues a reader. Telling too much can bore, as we saw in chapter 4. A wordy explanation can't tantalize the way an active, suggestive scene unfolding in real time can. Hints, unanswered questions, and fruitful ambiguity (as opposed to maddening opacity; no one likes that) can propel your work from the page to where all the best writing goes—the reader's memory.

In many cases, verbs spring from the personal, what you or I perceive and believe about events, actions, states, and existence. They are not physical things, not in the least bit concrete. A fox foraging in snow will leave tracks, but those are the imprints of the noun, not the verb. Verbs leave no material trace—nowhere, at least, but in the mind.

* * *

How do we suggest the ineffable through actions and dynamic verbs?

In the following exchange from *The Sound and the Fury*, William Faulkner wields the power of suggestion with extraordinary ease (and no punctuation). Minimal description, maximum heat. Quentin, the tormented young man who's narrating the scene, is grilling his sister, Caddy, about her boyfriend:

> do you love him Caddy
>
> do I what
>
> she looked at me then everything emptied out of her eyes and they looked like the eyes
>
> in the statues blank and unseeing and serene
>
> put your hand against my throat
>
> she took my hand and held it flat against her throat

now say his name

Dalton Ames

I felt the first surge of blood there it surged in strong accelerating beats

say it again . . .

her blood surged steadily beating and beating against my hand

Note that this intimate scene is *all action.* Emotions reveal themselves through actions but Faulkner leaves the emotions unnamed. Instead, he writes about what the conversation looks and feels like, how the characters behave, how their bodies respond. Readers' imaginations supply whatever they want to supply: what their subconscious delivers, what their experience fills in.

In laying out his corporeal stepping stones, Faulkner leads us to our own discovery of Caddy's and Quentin's feelings. We perceive them through Quentin's senses, through verbs that describe what he sees, hears, and feels. From his point of view, Caddy's reactions are forceful, as in "everything *emptied* out of her eyes." *Emptied*—what a surprising, visceral verb. More violent than *spilled. Emptied* feels like a sudden gushing whoosh, then nothingness. Her blood *surged*—also aggressive—"beating and beating against my hand": more than a little erotic. Yes, Faulkner goes there, or rather, he suggests powerful,

Suggest thoughts and feelings with dynamic verbs, rather than naming them outright.

possibly incestuous feelings. Quentin's view of Caddy's reactions opens up *his* state of mind.

For another example of the interpretive and suggestive quality of verbs, let's look at Patricia Highsmith's *The Two Faces of January*. Highsmith's domain is the psychological thriller; she's best known for the novels *Strangers on a Train* and *The Talented Mr. Ripley*, which inspired the well-known movies. Here, she takes us inside the minds and bodies of a con artist and his wife when a detective confronts them: "Chester's heart stumbled. . . . He looked at Colette and saw his own fear leap to her face . . ."

Stumbled: We read that and understand a heart wobbling in shock, an image that's unexpected yet clear. What Chester sees in Colette suggests her fight-or-flight response to sudden danger, and the reader can supply the rest—the blood draining from Colette's cheeks, perhaps, maybe a slight widening of her eyes. A lesser writer than Highsmith might have described the moment in those terms. But Highsmith hones the drama by putting us in Chester's head. We see what *he* sees through the lens of his anxiety, with an intensified awareness, seeing the act of leaping—his perception, and Highsmith's—in vacant, silent space.

What intense physical responses can you define with unusual but apt verbs, to suggest a fresh image?

You and I are Chester all day, every day, looking at life through our own lenses. Let's say you and your friend see a person wearing a backpack and boots, approaching a trailhead. If anyone quizzed the two of you, you'd both say she's a hiker, no question. But whether this person galumphed, ambled, or dragged herself up the trail is a matter of what subtleties her movement suggested to *you*. The verbs you'd use to describe the hiker's actions might be different from your friend's. They'd depend on how you gauged her effort and estimated her speed, what associations and memories her stride sparked in your mind.

Verbs mediate our experience; they link us to the world. In their vast variety, we have endless ways to express ourselves and understand our lives. Dynamic verbs aren't only for bold moves, but for clues and implications, too.

> To pack the Bud—oppose the Worm—
> Obtain its right of Dew—
> Adjust the Heat—elude the Wind—
> Escape the prowling Bee
>
> Great Nature not to disappoint
> Awaiting Her that Day—
> To be a Flower, is profound
> Responsibility—
>
> —EMILY DICKINSON, FROM
> "BLOOM—IS RESULT—TO MEET A FLOWER"

Dickinson emphasizes verbs throughout this poem (and her work in general). The theme would be quite different if she had written "*fight* the Worm / *Grab* its right of Dew." Instead, her verbs *oppose* and *obtain* signal that this flower is practical and conscientious, as it must be to benefit its community. In suggesting a reasonable frame of mind, the poet hints at a model for us as well.

Verbs exist in so many shades of connotation, expressing subtle feelings along with their primary meaning. As a result, they can suggest a great deal.

This makes verbs interesting and a little dangerous.

Imagine this exchange:

"I was *not* snickering."

"You were."

"Giggling, maybe."

"I distinctly heard you snicker."

"The verb you want, love, is *discerned.* No adverb needed."

"Snicker this."

Snicker, giggle: There's a slight difference in how those gurgly little eruptions *sound* coming out of someone's mouth, but a big difference in intention—and how we perceive it. Describe that not-quite-laughing with the wrong word and risk fireworks, because with such an abundant array of verbs, we're sensitive to their nuances.

Verbs can deliver the sass of a runway model and a good degree of brushoff. *Snicker? Chortle? Smirk?* So many options. Choose with care.

* * *

How do you want a reader to react to your writing? Verbs are how we convey meaning, so our verbs should relate to our purpose. Say you're writing about how someone is moving on foot. To amplify negative emotions, you might say the person would *crawl, stagger, limp, slog, trudge, drag, forge through.* But to get across ease and joy, you could have that character *dance, hop, scamper, bounce, slide, float, fly.* Or *dash, dart, jump, soar, sprint.*

In an explanatory, step-by-step piece of writing, more methodical verbs may work better: *start, walk through, think through, follow, watch for, end up.*

In chapter 2, I described verbs as the Cate Blanchetts of language, with their abilities to perform so many grammatical roles. Like Blanchett (one of my favorite actors), verbs are also supreme vehicles of expression. They're an entire art form, encompassing the vastness and detail of our experience.

But here's a caveat: A few verbs go a long way.

Typically, sentences contain more nouns than verbs. A pileup of nouns or adjectives, if written well, can fascinate and delight. That's not always the case with verbs. Too many can feel overwhelming. In a moment we'll look at ineffective and effective ways to string them together.

First, here's what I mean about the delight of nouns. Jay Gatsby is leading the woman he loves on a tour of his palatial home that ends in his bedroom, where he opens his closet:

> He took out a pile of shirts and began throwing them one by one before us, shirts of sheer linen and thick silk and fine flannel which lost their folds as they fell and covered the table in many-colored disarray. While we admired he brought more and the soft rich heap mounted higher—shirts with stripes and scrolls and plaids in coral and apple green and lavender and faint orange with monograms of Indian blue.

In a single paragraph bursting with textures and colors, Fitzgerald reveals Gatsby's overwhelming need to impress Daisy Buchanan with his wealth. After all, she'd rejected him years before because he lacked it. Gatsby makes her *feel* how rich he is—you can imagine the wind on her face from all that flying linen.

Yet a stream of verbs might not have the same luxurious effect. All those actions pushing at once can be tiring to read, and complicated to untangle. Experienced writers can make such mistakes, as in this snippet from prolific novelist Angela Thirkell, in *The Brandons*:

> Mr Grant did as he was told. As on a previous journey Mrs Brandon spoke very little, but this time her companion did not take her silence for scorn. To his adoration there began to be added a cooler admiration for someone who was going to do a job that not everyone would have done, and was doing it without any fuss.

Three forms of "to do" along with such needless passive-voice verbiage as "there began to be." The problem is not fancy verbs or frantic verbs; it's convoluted construction. "Was going to do" . . . "would have done" . . . "was doing"—these verb tenses complicate a simple point: Mr. Grant began to admire his friend for doing an unwanted job without complaint.

That passage also gets clogged up with noun forms of verbs—*adoration* instead of *adore*, *admiration* instead of *admire*. Thirkell *names* her character's emotions, rather than letting us *feel* them through his actions, whether visible or hidden in the body.

A sign at Mount Rainier National Park takes verb-loading to a humorous extreme:

> **DO NOT TREAD, MOSEY, HOP, TRAMPLE, STEP, PLOD, TIPTOE, TROT, TRAIPSE, MEANDER, CREEP, PRANCE, AMBLE, JOG, TRUDGE, MARCH, STOMP, TODDLE, JUMP, STUMBLE, TROD, SPRINT, OR WALK ON PLANTS.**

The point is clear. Rangers in the park's meadow restoration area aren't taking any chances.

Here's an excellent example of verb-loading, from Tim O'Brien's *The Things They Carried*, a piercing collection of stories about the Vietnam War and the damage it inflicted on mind and spirit. A soldier is about to take revenge on the medic he blames for keeping him out of action. Take a look at how O'Brien suggests his psychological state:

> I went back to my hootch, showered, shaved, threw my helmet against the wall, lay down for a while, got up, prowled around, talked to myself, applied some fresh ointment, then headed off to find Azar.

One active sentence, a multitude of inner injuries. The contradictory impulses of a young man bent on brutality come through in this rapid-fire list brimming with precise verbs. Precise but not fancy. These are fairly ordinary actions. They gain drama and emotion through O'Brien's swift pace and the way he slips hostility into the routine. The soldier grooms himself like someone's well-bred son yet he's also out of control, raging, hurling his helmet. He rests but then he prowls, an animal on the hunt. He talks to himself—a sign, perhaps, of wavering confidence and strain. The fussy ritual of wound care (ointment *applied*, not smeared or slapped on) recalls the physical weakness that has embarrassed him and also suggests a methodical mind shifting into gear.

The example illustrates that *how* writers use verbs is just as important as what verbs they use. O'Brien's style is straightforward but it produces a profound emotional effect.

What can we learn from this?

No need for fancy verbs.

Simple verbs can be enough.

Motion verbs suggest internal states more efficiently than lengthy, wordy descriptions.

Also, constraints can lead to creativity, as Faulkner demonstrates in what two people can say with gestures, as Highsmith proves in what two people can say without words *or* gestures, and as

O'Brien shows in what one person can go through all alone in his hootch.

A few sharp actions may be all it takes to create a magnificent scene.

* * *

Good Habits

To suggest a character's thoughts and feelings instead of describing them explicitly, think of an emotion and write a short narrative (100–150 words) that illustrates the emotion with verbs.

For example: Suspicion

> Her eyes narrowed and her throat clenched as she hunted through his texts, scouring his words for hidden signs of betrayal. She replayed the moments in her mind. He'd lied about every delay; someone else had lured him away from her, promising him fixes, cash, and more.

Use your imagination to replace some of those verbs with uncommon ones.

How would you suggest other emotions—regret, jealousy, desire, etc.—through behaviors and action? Write, too, about the emotions you don't quite understand and can't name, the ones that confuse and perplex.

Keep in mind the emotional effect that different verbs close in meaning can have on your reader (in the example above, *scouring* as opposed to *reading*).

CHAPTER 7

Notice

Tips on capturing movement to pull readers into your story. Defy AI with poetic use of verbs.

She seemed to be wearing the sunlight, rearranging it around her from time to time, with a movement of one hand, with a movement of her head, and with her smile—

—JAMES BALDWIN, *THE DEVIL FINDS WORK*

Close observation is such an important part of writing. I suppose that's why I write. The way people speak, interact, and move fascinates me.

We learn a great deal about people—and the characters we read about—from the way they move (or don't). A person's carriage and way of taking up space telegraphs how he feels inside, his spirit, self regard, and habit. Past experiences and present purpose braid through one's posture.

By describing a character's movements with vivid verbs and tying these movements into larger themes, writers can draw readers deeper into their stories. In the Tim O'Brien excerpt we considered at the end of chapter 6, a few sharp, staccato verbs make us *feel* a soldier's anguish and the tug-of-war in his mind. In the passage from reporter Eli Saslow's story in chapter 1, verbs reveal the struggles and defiant pride of a woman living on food stamps. They bring us into her world.

We crave a living connection with others. Nonverbal expression binds us powerfully, in ways we may not even realize. As a dance critic, I've paid special attention to this. I have to think a lot about the hows and whys of nonverbal expression when I'm analyzing a dance. And I also have to heed my own physical responses to it.

Here's an example. The Alvin Ailey American Dance Theater, a prominent modern-dance company, often ends its shows with an exhilarating, gospel-themed whirlwind of a dance called *Revelations*. The dance depicts an episodic journey to a riverside baptism, with side trips into doubt and damnation, and watching it you feel the pull of urgent truth. There's nothing especially fancy about the dancers' steps, though it takes extraordinary technique to perform them. Their movements are strong and clear, with high kicks and torsos arcing backward, the body knocked off its axis by a holy spirit. A sense of fiery abandon builds, the dancers spiral and sail, their heat spills into the audience, and at the end, without fail, spectators jump from their seats in rapture.

But the part that moves me to tears is a quiet little moment when almost nothing happens.

It comes just before the big finale, as the first notes ripple in "Rocka My Soul in the Bosom of Abraham." The men—dressed at this point in trousers and vests—step toward their partners and offer an elbow, as if to say, "Hey there! Care to join me?"

That's it—the step, the gallant elbow, and suddenly I'm seeing blurry. What follows is a dipping, swaying, spinning folk dance, legs swinging, arms reaching; the group breaks into diverging lines but the music pulls them back together until they're all pivoting from point to point in unison like one body, one spirit.

But it all starts with a gesture.

Why does that get me? It's the sweetness, the care. It feels genuine and artless, easy as breathing. A glimpse of social harmony.

Casual sweetness opens me up whenever I see it, in the grocery store, at the library, in the parking lot where just the other day a stranger vaulted to stop a runaway cart from adding to the dents on my car.

Some folks offer joy in motion just walking down the street with buoyant ease, and I feel it, too.

Have you ever been drawn to a person by the way they smiled at you on the sidewalk? Maybe they also sidestepped into a driveway with their bulldog straining at his leash, allowing you to pass by unslobbered.

Goodbye, my heart.

I remember a barista whose stillness cooled my nerves. I was standing at the counter in mid-brainfreeze. I'd left three hungry kids in the car after promising to return with coffee-shop goodies, but here I was unable to choose. A line formed behind me—maybe fifteen seconds passed, maybe an hour—and my insides churned under imagined waves of judgment. What must all those supple and decisive Portlanders be thinking?

I blinked at the barista and saw on his face an attitude of dry, quiet patience. Grounded in the early morning mist of milk foam and mood swings, he seemed to telegraph that he would wait all day, no worries, my carbs mattered. Brain fog didn't faze him. The man's motor ran at a leisurely rpm, and calmed my own. I left with forgettable pastries; what lasted was his grace.

* * *

Watching someone else move triggers our own sensorimotor systems in subtle ways; we sense their actions in our bodies. Similarly, reading about a person's movement stimulates our natural, empathetic ability to feel the actions and emotions of those around us. Small details of behavior tickle our sensitivities as we read, breathing air into the intangibles of human connection. Yet writers often overlook the expressive possibilities in their characters' movement.

> The unpracticed novelist cleaves to the static because it is much easier to describe than the mobile: it is getting these people out of the aspic of arrest and mobilized in a scene that is hard.
>
> —JAMES WOOD, *HOW FICTION WORKS*

To be sure, static images are easier to describe than moving ones. It may seem enough to freeze a character in the mind's eye and note her hair color, height and weight, heels or sneakers. But remember the deliciousness of the power of suggestion. And nothing's more suggestive than flesh in motion. Let go of the wall, kick into the deep end, and submerge yourself in the verby waters of how your protagonist moves through a scene, her world, her life.

Does she hold her breastbone just so, mindful of the drape of her pashmina?

Where is the locus of sassitude—in a purposeful stride with criss-crossing thighs or the swish of a backside? In drifting barefoot along a gravel path? Show your readers a liberated spirit through a liberated body.

The body speaks its own language. We translate it best through verbs because we are made of movement, from dividing cells to beating heart to the ability to silence conversation by tripping over the carpet and diving into the cheese board, glasses flying as olives bounce and the Boursin smears on the sofa.

* * *

I once interviewed Rita Moreno, the dancer, singer, and Oscar-winning actor, about the lack of movement awareness in so many contemporary film stars. What do they miss by ignoring the physical dimension of a character? Her answer addressed acting but applies equally to writing.

"If you can find a way your character moves," Moreno said, "you know more about your character than you'd ever dream."

Great writers excel at capturing mobility and—of course—the key is accurate verbs. George Orwell's *Down and Out in Paris and London*, a memoir of his early years as a dishwasher, sweeps along with the vigor of his action verbs. They bolster a theme of his book: Hunger and privation exist and they cause misery, but they haven't beaten him down. He is wrestling with them, and his lively mind and body remain ever alert. In the passage below, Orwell watches a waiter transform himself. All he's doing is passing from kitchen to dining room, but Orwell sees magic: "The set of his shoulders alters; all the dirt and hurry and irritation have dropped off in an instant. He glides over the carpet, with a solemn priest-like air."

What a performance: waiter as actor, dancer, magician, master of self-presentation. From head to toe, he snaps into alignment at the change of setting. In Orwell's verbs—*dropped off, glides*—we feel the rebirth of this man, striding through cooking fumes to bestow grace upon the public.

At another point, Orwell describes an assistant maître d'hôtel halting at the kitchen door to tear into an apprentice, yelling and "shaking his fist above his head." Then he entered the dining room "and sailed across it dish in hand, graceful as a swan. Ten seconds later he was bowing reverently to a customer." The verbs wing along with the descriptions—what he carried, how he moved, how fast—to pitch the reader into the action. Orwell's world of fellow survivors swirls with motion and resilience. It hums with a celebration of life.

* * *

How does a writer take the first steps to accomplish this, recording the mobile moment? People-watching is free entertainment and crucial education. Let strangers school your eye: That fellow who reins in his step to glower at fellow passersby—what's eating him? Who has the airiest presence, the floating stride that makes you wonder about her sport, her job, and the source of the silkiness that ribbons through her bones? Some couples walking together convey ease, others melancholy; how do their bodies express the difference?

Imagine a woman walking—no, bopping—across a courtyard. Her hips swing, curls bounce, bracelets chime. With a whoop she greets a friend at a table and sweeps her into an embrace. Her momentum knocks both of them into a radical tilt. Her friend's iced tea spills, but our subject makes no move to sop it up. Exuberance pours from her, but is there also a hint of self-absorption, a quest to make a big deal of herself at the expense of others? We sympathize with the quiet, patient friend who's sitting in wet shorts.

Or might the writer's further revelation show us something else: that the loose-limbed hugger is, in fact, struggling to regulate herself. She's weaning off her meds, and while barging around comes naturally, seeing what's going on around her doesn't, not yet. Our sympathies shift. Charged physical language opens up storytelling possibilities, leading our curiosity one way and another.

* * *

In 2019 the Washington Nationals won the World Series, their first championship in franchise history. The DC area lost its mind. I did, too. Enraptured by these joyful underdogs with their fun walk-up music and dugout dances, I wrote some brief movement sketches. The great grunting pitcher Max Scherzer especially intrigued me. He could fail and fail and still find a way to sort through the mess and win. As I watched him claw a victory out of Game 1, I fixed on the tremendous force of that elongated multidirectional body and how quickly it reorganized itself. This told me something about Scherzer:

> Pitch after pitch, Scherzer's big body flew apart, like a rubber doll wrenched by a maniac's hands: torso snapped in half, right leg kicking out to third base, left knee horribly torqued. But those eyes locked forward, watching his sliders, and sometimes watching his hopes die. The star simply got back to business. Scherzer gathered his exploded joints back together and set up for the next ordeal.

Watching athletes is an excellent place to start experimenting with writing about movement. Verbs zoom to mind because the actions are so extreme. Writers of any kind of material, fact or fiction, can learn about verbs from sportswriters. Sally Jenkins of *The Washington Post* is one of my favorites. Here's a typical gem, in her column about the WNBA's Caitlin Clark, of the Indiana Fever, playing against the Atlanta Dream in her rookie season. To frame her theme about the danger of underestimating this star, Jenkins points up Clark's ability to fake out her opponents:

> Clark dribbled strongly to her right—got [Dream defender Maya] Caldwell to commit—then abruptly flushed the ball backward, cut hard, recovered the dribble with her left hand for a crossover behind the back at full sprint and larked freely into an open layup. All while Caldwell whirled around confusedly.

Larked freely into an open layup—what a clear, dramatic image. A body in its athletic prime gives rise to such vivid images.

So can an aging, raging ballplayer, even if the drama is of a different sort. In a classic account of the immortal Ty Cobb in his seventies, sportswriter Al Stump casts an unflinching eye:

> Cobb despised the medical profession.
>
> At the same time, his sense of balance was almost gone. He tottered about the lodge, moving from place to place by grasping the furniture. On any public street, he couldn't navigate 20 feet without clutching my shoulder, leaning most of his 208 pounds upon me and shuffling along at a spraddle-legged gait.

In this profile for *True* magazine, Stump continues with Cobb's agonizing difficulties in the bathroom and his pill-gulping habit. Cobb guessed at the doses because many of the bottles had lost their labels. The description breaks your heart because despite his pain, Cobb refused the hospital. With strong, visceral verbs, Stump shows us what Cobb's suffering looks and feels like: the heat of his fever, his moans. Reading how he stuffed himself with pills, my own throat rebels. These behaviors draw me into the maddening and poignant tragedy of a combative, obstinate man who once was a god, still sees himself as a god, and fears that asking for help will deny his own existence.

This is what Anton Chekhov was getting at when he wrote to his brother: "Be sure not to discuss your hero's state of mind. Make it clear from his actions."

* * *

This brings me to another argument for finessing your writing with the right verbs.

AI may be pounding on the writer's door. But the writer has some defenses. AI cannot do what you can do to make your work *unforgettable*: Surprise the reader. Write with truthfulness and humanity. Write with fresh verbs.

I'm not Pollyannaish enough to believe that journalism, literature, marketing content, and other forms of writing can easily resist the onslaught of bots. Countless news organizations and other employers of writers are relying on the word production and hallucinations of AI even though they also require human writers to fix them—the so-called AI babysitters. Here's a grim testimonial about where that leads: "I contributed to a lot of the garbage that's filling the internet and destroying it," a writer told the BBC after he lost his job rewriting AI-generated articles for a tech company. "Nobody was even reading this stuff by the time I left because it's just trash."

He's right. It's distressing and everywhere: bad summaries, flat, uninformative explanations. Here's a typical example. I searched "how to use perambulate in a sentence" and landed on a site that offered many paragraphs of fluff before this instruction: *Begin your sentence with a subject, like "He" or "She." Follow the subject with the verb "perambulate" to indicate the action of walking or traveling.*

AI content tends to run to what I'm arguing against: numbing obviousness, lack of nuance, forgettable phrasing, clichés and lifeless metaphors, telling not showing, no personality.

I asked ChatGPT to write a love scene between talking trout in a mountain brook using all active verbs. The result began like this:

> In the crystal-clear waters of the mountain brook, two trout, Trevor and Tessa, swam gracefully, their scales shimmering like precious jewels in the dappled sunlight. Their hearts danced to the rhythm of the babbling stream as they circled each other, their fins brushing in a tender caress.

> Trevor darted forward with a flick of his tail, his eyes locking onto Tessa's with an intensity that stirred her very core. With a graceful twist, Tessa mirrored his movements, their bodies intertwining in a graceful ballet of desire.

Because this is a family verb book, I am sparing you the story's end, which got too hot for this babbling stream and threatened to cook the other fish who were undoubtedly begging Trevor and Tessa to slip behind a rock somewhere.

However, these two paragraphs are enough. Three mentions of gracefulness; hearts dancing (?), and a parallelism problem in the last sentence. (Better: With a graceful twist, Tessa mirrored his movements, *her body* intertwining with his . . .) Not to get too picky, but how *do* fish intertwine? That takes more gymnastics than simple entwining. I'm imagining slippery looped figure eights. Also, I note that neither trout talks. Did Big C not read the prompt?

(I realize I wrote that in my teaching voice, the one murmuring in my head as I grade papers. Chat, my friend, please find me during office hours.)

I decided to give it another try, and asked for a five-paragraph short story using strong active verbs about two alligators planning brunch, interrupted by a surprise guest. As animal stories go, this one is more tolerable than the fish romantasy. ChatGPT, eager to impress, produced seven paragraphs. The first two:

> In the heart of the Louisiana bayou, two alligators, Al and Gus, were planning their Sunday brunch extravaganza. Al snapped up some succulent crawfish while Gus wrestled with a hefty catfish, their mouths watering in anticipation. They squabbled over recipes, their tails swishing in excitement as they concocted their culinary masterpiece.
>
> As they debated the perfect seasoning for their gumbo, a

> rustle in the reeds interrupted their fervent planning. With a flick of their tails, they turned to find an unexpected guest—a majestic heron named Henrietta, her sleek feathers shimmering in the sunlight. Al and Gus exchanged puzzled glances, unsure of how to react to this uninvited visitor.

You get the idea. Predictable adjectives, yes. Active verbs, check. More tail-flicking, just like Trevor, the horny trout! What a limited vocabulary AI has. This passage is also a bit stereotypical, though maybe I'm reading too much into the names. I do like "squabbled over recipes." But in the same breath Al and Gus are also happily collaborating on a masterpiece. So they're *not* squabbling? Rethink that verb. This author, obviously, has never been around alligators, has it?

Here's what I know about alligators. A few years ago, one charged at me and next thing I knew I was inside my car with no memory of how I got there. My lizard brain did all the work. All I remember is that long blade of a body shooting across the creek, popping up on my side, and blinding me with its stare.

Even a brunching gator needs some bossassery.

Defy AI with your originality, your human senses, your fleshly experience of this world. Open your imagination to truth, energy, and drama.

AI can generate better text than it did in those brief exercises above. But what AI cannot do is think explicitly about its living self. It cannot watch the light in summer and feel it as a type of motion, as

Zadie Smith does with such grace in *Swing Time*, when she describes an afternoon among tomato plants:

> The garden was long and thin and it faced south, the outhouse abutted the right-hand fence, so you could watch the sun fall behind it, rippling the air as it went.

No bot—so far—can craft poetic physical language that makes us feel something. That is your territory. You can surprise and move your reader with your own irreplaceable sensitivity, your necessary nervous system, and your deliberate, intentional, refreshing verbs to connect it all.

* * *

Good Habits

- Here's an exercise combining the power of suggestion from chapter 6 with the drama of nonverbal expressions we explored in this chapter. Imagine you're in a crowded bar where a live band is playing and folks are starting to dance. ("Would field research help?" you ask. Oh *yes*, always a good idea.) You watch as people find partners, bop and sway, switch partners, sidle away, prowl, preen. Quite a floor show! You can't hear conversations but there's plenty of body language. What does it tell you?
- Ignite the scene with verbs and images to show the dynamics and suggest emotions. What actions large or small—lingering glances or rebuffed invitations, for example—convey the humor or poignancy? Challenge yourself to find vivid, specific verbs that reveal the characters' personalities and thoughts. Have fun whipping up backstories and next steps.

- Practice bringing another location to life with vivid verbs. Pick a space with physical activity. For instance, a restaurant kitchen, where the meat cook slings brisket toward the servers, the saucier swirls risotto with one hand and jolts his sauté pan with the other, and the line cooks swivel from slicing to stirring.
- You might start with where you work, a favorite gathering place with friends, or where you exercise or play a sport. You could also dream up a hotel lobby where fictional characters meet, or a crowded beach. To start, list the behaviors, movement patterns, and quick little incidents that you think might make a lively scene.
- Now that you've got your list, where can you find the tension, humor, and revealing details to animate the scene? Armed with these observations, write a passage with sharp, specific verbs that show the turmoil and excitement.

CHAPTER 8

Zhuzh It Up

Add style and spirit with metaphors and similes that refuse to sit still. Breathe life into landscapes with metaphorical verbs.

The terrible low sky strangles the daybreak.

—JUAN RAMÓN JIMÉNEZ, *PLATERO AND I*

As a sculptor turns to clay, and a choreographer to movement, the writer turns to language. Words possess as many expressive possibilities and as much flexibility as plasticine or dancers. As you write, you'll cultivate a feel for the language that suits your purpose—straightforward and concise, descriptive and lush, attuned to emotions, rich in symbolism, intimate, cool, elevated, and so on. This is how a writer develops a style.

But no writer starts from scratch. Literary devices abound to help unlock the creative potential of language. In this chapter we'll explore some of the finest literary devices: metaphors and similes. They combine brevity with élan, especially when they crackle with dynamic verbs.

Think of metaphor as a stellar collision. Two ideas crash and, *boom*, there's a burst of insight.

"So we beat on, boats against the current, borne back ceaselessly into the past."

We are not boats, but this doesn't stop Fitzgerald, in his remarkable last line of *The Great Gatsby*, from equating us with them. In the introduction to this book, I laid out my argument for the lyrical power of Fitzgerald's verbs in this sentence. Here, I want to zero in on how the verbs add to the grace of his metaphor.

Fitzgerald's choice of verbs—*beat on* and *borne back*—expresses an unending cycle of human nature, as we strive and return, always returning, drifting back to a time of hope. Those verbs also lend the image a certain gentleness. *Beat on* suggests to me a spiritual inevitability, a heartbeat and the light physical action of bobbing, the way boats nose into a rippling, rhythmic current. That softness and the sympathetic tone: This verb-driven image comes from an understanding soul. It's poignant and luminous, specific and meaningful in a way no other, wordier description can match.

The verb-centricity of Fitzgerald's metaphor also sets it apart. In equating two different things to brighten or enliven each other, metaphors often take the form A is B. Time is money. The world is your oyster. To be sure, these metaphors are efficient, effective, and enduring (though too common to be of much use in your writing). Even so, metaphors can shoot in many directions. When dynamic verbs drive them forward, they can deliver an almost physical force that intensifies emotion.

* * *

Similes are another powerful literary device, comparing two unlike things, often in a phrase beginning with *like* or *as*. As with metaphors, overuse has thinned many similes into clichés: Run like the wind. Fight like hell.

The world needs your fresh similes!

In his autobiography *My Life and Hard Times*, the humorist and cartoonist James Thurber describes a host of calamities that rained upon his childhood in Columbus, Ohio, at the turn of the twentieth century. This one occurred the night someone parked the family car too far from the curb. (Italics are mine.)

> The first streetcar that came along couldn't get by. It *picked up the tired old automobile as a terrier might seize a rabbit* and drubbed it unmercifully, losing its hold now and then but catching a new grip a second later. Tires booped and whooshed, the fenders queeled and graked, the steering wheel *rose up like a spectre* and disappeared in the direction of Franklin Avenue with a melancholy whistling sound, bolts and gadgets *flew like sparks from a Catherine wheel.* It was a splendid spectacle.

Splendid indeed. Motion verbs and similes drive Thurber's account. They plunge us into chaos and drama, showing us the agonies of a car that isn't just a car but a defenseless pet. Thurber also tosses in specific details, heightening our emotional involvement: a street name, various car parts flying in space. It is all pictures, pathos, and noise. The streetcar is a beast on a tear and you feel it plow into the stranded auto, yanking it around and mashing it to pieces. The tempo races with eccentric verbs and wordplay. *Whooshed* is a proper onomatopoeic verb, but other verbs Thurber uses have no entries in the *Oxford English Dictionary*. *Booped*, *queeled*, and *graked* seem to be self-coined Thurber accents to a wild, witty symphony of ruin.

Metaphors and similes paint pictures in the mind. Their verbs stimulate feeling; they add a flash of originality and style. And they can make your meaning clearer than a dry, ordinary explanation.

The witty essayist Robert Benchley relied on metaphor in his

Craft verb-driven metaphors and similes to boost the drama, add pizzazz, and rev up emotion.

1933 satire about the disappearance of a type of prairie chicken known as the heath hen (whose extinction seems to have been reversed in 1998, hooray!): "It was not enough that *the world should be tottering, its reason going,* its standards gone." (Italics are mine.)

What a vivid, onomatopoeic verb, *totter.* With its internal consonance of repeated *t*'s, the word itself sounds rocky and clackety, like something on the brink of collapse. Al Stump used it to describe an elderly Ty Cobb, in the excerpt in chapter 7. Benchley's figurative use of the verb here has a very different texture, and expresses two things at once: the kookiness of a planet off its axis and the high-spirited, pseudo-serious tone of the writer.

Our world is not only screwballing around in space, Benchley continues, it's losing its mind, its principles. Wow. What a thing. Wait, are we . . . ? Why, yes, I believe we're still tottering. Girl, the world is tottering like crazy. All these years later, Benchley's image is funny, sad, and timeless.

* * *

The possibilities are endless for trenchant and potent verb-driven metaphors, similes, and figures of speech. Poets and songwriters know their power:

> You may trod me in the very dirt
> But still, like dust, I'll rise.
>
> —MAYA ANGELOU, "STILL I RISE"

Trod, past tense of *tread*, lands a punch in Angelou's defiant poem. *Trod* has the weight of *trample* in a single, blunt syllable. It also means crushing or oppressing someone by force—Angelou's larger point. Her theme of nimble resilience comes in the next line. The perfect verb captures it.

> The river sweats
> Oil and tar
>
> —T. S. ELIOT, "THE WASTE LAND," PART 3, "THE FIRE SERMON"

> The beach hisses like fat.
>
> —ELIZABETH BISHOP, "SANDPIPER"

In these lines, living actions surprise the brain and animate the environment. With quick, crisp verbs we see polluted waters glisten and hear seafoam bubble on sand. Try replacing *sweats* and *hisses* with other verbs: The river oozes? Exudes? Nope. The poets' choices click.

> . . . the trees
> Shook out their shadows in the breeze
> which carried half the sky away.
>
> —ELIZABETH JENNINGS, "THE SHOT"

How do you paint a picture of air? *Moving* air? Jennings studied the shadows on grass and the clouds above, and by invoking their actions with vigorous verbs (*shake out*, *carry away*) she leads readers to visualize the breeze and feel its sweep.

> Until the rainbow burns the stars out in the sky (Always)
> Until the ocean covers every mountain high (Always)
> Until the dolphin flies and parrots live at sea . . .
>
> —STEVIE WONDER, "AS"

Impossible actions fill this song, symbolizing the impossibility of love's ever dying. Rainbows and dolphins delight the mind's eye, but it's their actions that express the theme of an everlasting bond.

* * *

Start by noticing verb-driven images and figures of speech all around you, and discovering what you like. Listen to songs, read with your senses tuned to the efficient and apt figure of speech. (Find tips on creating your own metaphors at the end of this chapter.)

Metaphors do more than illustrate. With a strong subject and verb they can turn abstract concepts into fleshy, vigorous things we see and feel. Take a look:

> Falsehood flies, and Truth comes limping after it.
>
> —JONATHAN SWIFT, *THE EXAMINER #14,* "THE ART OF POLITICAL LYING"

> She could feel the countless hands of habit dragging her back into some fresh compromise with fate.
>
> —EDITH WHARTON, *THE HOUSE OF MIRTH*

> Her welter of apologies reminds me of why I prefer difficult stars, the ones who barricade themselves inside their stardom and spit through the cracks.
>
> —JENNIFER EGAN, *A VISIT FROM THE GOON SQUAD*

These metaphors personify lies, truth, habit, and stardom—but that's not all. They shine a light on specific qualities: the speed at which lies spread, the way force of habit can thwart the will. And the fortress that fame offers, if you happen to be the kind of celebrity who's fed up with her adoring public.

* * *

Think in metaphors and similes, and you'll find you can intensify emotion and drama all around. You can feel the ocean boil or a mountain suffer. Metaphorical verbs breathe life into a landscape.

Open vistas, cramped canyons, urban alleys, dark interiors: These can be a writer's playground. But using space effectively takes more than describing what a scene looks like as if you're staging a photo shoot. With imagination and dynamic verbs, you can design metaphorical language that plays with the setting so it quivers with life. Expressing motion—whether implied or explicit—in your landscape allows you to shape your reader's perception, direct her attention, and prompt her to feel a certain way.

In Ray Bradbury's *The Martian Chronicles*, the red planet is no barren rock but a lively place where you see "the baked hills simmering down into frosty night," and the soil is "so black and shiny it almost crawled and stirred in your fist."

Bradbury injects action into the landscape and *shows* us what kind of place this is—rather than telling us with static description. Is the Martian terrain peaceful and pleasant? Not at all. This hilly land is uneasy and more than a little creepy, in a specific, palpable way. (Something inanimate wiggling around in the fingers, eww . . .)

A writhing, heaving setting also suggests a metaphysical quality. A landscape or even a built interior space that feels active and alive seems to defy the laws of nature. The setting becomes a character, and the writer gives herself more territory on which to develop theme, meaning, and emotion.

Use dramatic action verbs to deepen your descriptions of setting and fill them with emotion.

The elegant Victorian-era mystery writer Wilkie Collins, so generous with detail and sensitive to rhythm, wove powerful atmospheric descriptions through his novels. There's a sense that the whole *spirit* of a place is in on the villainy. *The Moonstone*, his 1868 whodunit, centers on the theft of a renowned Indian diamond from a rambling English estate where suspects abound. Collins inserts so much menace into a stretch of nearby shoreline that *it* feels like a suspect, too:

> The sand-hills here run down to the sea, and end in two spits of rock jutting out opposite each other, till you lose sight of them in the water. One is called the North Spit, and one the South. Between the two, shifting backwards and forwards at certain seasons of the year, lies the most horrible quicksand on the shores of Yorkshire. At the turn of the tide, something goes on in the unknown deeps below, which sets the whole face of the quicksand shivering and trembling in a manner most remarkable to see, and which has given to it, among the people in our parts, the name of the Shivering Sand. . . . A lonesome and a horrid retreat, I can tell you! No boat ever ventures into this bay. No children from our fishing-village, called Cobb's Hole, ever come here to play. The very birds of the air, as it seems to me, give the Shivering Sand a wide berth.

This sea isn't passively hemmed by sand-hills. Collins could have described the hills as "near the sea," or he could have written, just as mildly, that they border the sea. He could have accepted their stationary quality and moved on, but instead he animates them, and they join the mysterious world of his story. Likewise, the spits of rock don't just sit there, existing, and neither does the sand; instead, the rock juts out and the hills of sand "run down." Collins immerses us in the scene as his narrator addresses us directly. We feel his urgency; he's almost imploring us to gird ourselves against this threatening supernatural action that never stops. Something horrible is going on in those sinister deeps—and like the quicksand, we almost feel a shiver.

* * *

A half century later, E. M. Forster brings us even closer to the spiritual life of a natural setting in the opening of his 1924 novel *A Passage to India*. He marshals the trees rising above the city of Chandrapore (now Chandrapur) to begin laying out his theme:

> On the second rise is laid out the little civil station, and viewed hence Chandrapore appears to be a totally different place. It is a city of gardens. It is no city, but a forest sparsely scattered with huts. It is a tropical pleasaunce washed by a noble river. The toddy palms and neem trees and mangoes and pepul that were hidden behind the bazaars now become visible and in their turn hide the bazaars. They rise from the gardens where ancient tanks nourish them, they burst out of stifling purlieus and unconsidered temples. Seeking light and air, and endowed with more strength than man or his works, they soar above the lower deposit to greet one another with branches and beckoning leaves, and to build a city for the birds. Especially after the rains do they screen what passes below, but at all times, even when scorched or leafless, they glorify the city to the English

> people who inhabit the rise, so that new-comers cannot believe it to be as meagre as it is described, and have to be driven down to acquire disillusionment.

The trees, with names that place us in a specific part of the world, shape the view with active motion: hiding the bazaar, rising, bursting out, screening. They also model virtuous living. They seek the life-giving essentials of light and air and—Forster emphasizes this—the intangibles that give life meaning. They bond and help others (soaring "to greet one another . . . and to build a city for the birds"). These are spiritual qualities, and in this description I hear the echo of Forster's vigorous "only connect" credo from his earlier novel *Howards End*: "Only connect! That was the whole of her sermon. Only connect the prose and the passion, and both will be exalted, and human love will be seen at its height. Live in fragments no longer."

In *A Passage to India,* Forster contrasts the vigorous trees with their human counterparts as he caps this remarkable description with a single verb: *glorify*. "They glorify the city to the English people who inhabit the rise," he writes, "so that new-comers cannot believe it to be as meagre as it is described . . ."

Glorify—a rich verb, used here with irony. It signals a shift in Forster's perspective, from how *he* sees the trees to how the new arrivals see them, as decor for their life on the rise. This novel, like *The Moonstone*, takes place during the British raj, and both books grapple with the costs of imperialism. Forster begins to limn the costs with his forest metaphor, right at the start.

Before we leave this excerpt, notice the passive voice in the last sentence: Outsiders see the full picture only if they are "driven down." The author, emphasizing the visitors' separateness, leaves their drivers nameless. This is only the second paragraph of his novel, but with powerful verbs, Forster distills the chief tensions of his book: the gulf between colonizers and the colonized, and between men and the land they strive to conquer.

* * *

Activating natural surroundings isn't just for literary giants, however. This fascinating sentence comes from a nineteenth-century geology journal:

> We never enjoyed a pipe half so much as when solitarily disinterring organic remains which had slumbered in the heart of the rock for myriads of ages.

Disinterring in any other context would seem like a grim activity; here the writer pairs it with *enjoyed.* I read it again and pause on *slumbered,* a peaceful act that anchors the image. It calls to mind hibernating bears and pleasant dreams. To slumber is to rest, and the verb prompts the reader to empathize with those ancient remains and their hidden, possibly violent history—remains that for all these long years have rested in peace.

The writer's use of *slumber* confers a quality of gentleness upon him and his actions as well. I picture him taking care with the remains to which he's given a characteristic of life. I see his respect for their delicate state—*disinterring* them, implying a careful process, rather than, say, the roughness of *digging up* or *excavating.* These verbs paint a portrait. Here is a thoughtful scientist in his element, alongside a companion while *enjoying*—another resonant verb—a pipe, perhaps the apex of relaxation.

To deepen and expand your writing, seek out the behaviors of nature. Does a mountain view sweep you clean? How do you feel when the wind slaps, clouds foam, or your houseplants rally? Embody the living world in your imagination and enliven it on the page. Potent verbs and verbals invigorate this stanza of "The Hermit," by the eighteenth-century Irish poet Thomas Parnell:

> But now the Clouds in airy Tumult fly,
> The Sun emerging opes an azure Sky;
> A fresher green the smelling Leaves display,
> And glitt'ring as they tremble, cheer the Day . . .

Parnell's point: Better to immerse ourselves in the raw mess of life than to barricade against it, like a hermit. He sees a model in the soaring renewal of the natural world, hailing each morning's fresh start. Cheer the day: What brighter, more attainable first step? What sweeter call to optimism?

* * *

Good Habits

To invent fresh, active similes and metaphors, try these exercises:

- **Rewrite the metaphors** I've listed in this chapter with your own nouns and verbs. Pour out your thoughts: crazy things, utter nonsense, the first words that pop to mind. Remember that metaphors arise from two ideas crashing to reveal new insight. Can you enliven the lines with a different crash? Surprise your brain with contrasts. Keep these in a file or notebook of metaphors to inspire you when you need them.
- **Visualize a scene** you're writing about in terms of big, exaggerated actions. Say you're crafting a tense conversation. You see tension filling the room. Swap in a more dramatic

verb: Tension floods the room. From there, imagine tension rising like a river, barreling forth and drowning out the peace. Build on the image, play with it to shape a metaphor with emotional force.

- **Think of the telling actions** of an object or person. Do these behaviors suggest phrases you can use in a simile? Recall the times you've felt high emotions or witnessed something unusual. Here's one of my memories: watching a masseur roll and press an athlete's muscles *like a baker kneading dough.* Add your phrases to the file I suggested above, even if you have no use for the similes now. Keeping the fragments on hand is better than straining to come up with an image in the moment, as you stare at your screen.
- **Brainstorm word associations** about everyday events. Remember that metaphors and similes steer clear of physical truth; the aim is emotional truth. Does your head ever ache like it's full of loose change and banging against the wall? Is the sunset spilling wine? Blurt out the words, write them down to save for when you need them. With practice, seeing (and feeling) things this way gets easier.

CHAPTER 9

Cigarette Me

Why new verbs catch fire—and who leads the language changes.

I like the feeling of words doing as they want to do and as they have to do.

—GERTRUDE STEIN, *PAINTED LACE, AND OTHER PIECES, 1914–1937*

"Where do you summah?" Ben Bradlee, the former executive editor of *The Washington Post*, asked me in his Bostonian accent, dripping with money. I blinked into my wineglass and tried to look as if I were sorting through glamorous options.

One of us must have been tipsy. Or perhaps I'd succeeded in impersonating someone accustomed to schmoozing at tony Georgetown soirees. I may be the partying kind, but I do not summer.

One summers in the Hamptons, or the Vineyard, or possibly Biarritz, though I may be wrong about that. Is Biarritz for wintering? Or autumning? Whatever the season, that spot sounds divine. Yet if travelers springed or falled there, the grammar police would drag them in for questioning.

English is a living, evolving language, and among its most amusing—and misunderstood—evolutions is the way nouns morph into verbs. We saw how verbs become nouns (called verbal nouns) in chapter 2. Here we'll explore the flipside. We'll look at how and why these innovative verbs catch on and who pushes them forward.

Nouns change to verbs with ease, generally following the same grammatical rules as other verbs. Cooks ladle, steam, and zest; chemists oxygenate and acidify. In the newsroom, editors workshop headlines and proof pages. For a minute in the '80s, I permed my hair, oversized my jackets, and corset-belted everything (because it was all so *big*).

But if you find that some noun-verb mutations grate, I'm right there with you. Many folks have strong opinions about such verb mutations. I have a few of those, too. So first a little venting.

For instance, you won't catch me nunc pro tuncing anything. That's a legal term meaning "now for then," used to correct something after the fact, and believe it or not it oozes forth now and then as an incomprehensible verb freak. I weep inside when I hear it, which is not often, but you never know, do you, when otherwise pleasant people may take it upon themselves to strut around nunc pro tuncing this or that, and there goes everything.

I'm averse to strings of syllables masquerading as a quality word. *Securitize*, say, or *functionalize*. (Why not simply *make it work*? Fewer syllables!) *Deconfessionalize*—gack. With a complicated idea like that—it means removing religious influence—I prefer a clear explanation to a convoluted verbal pretzel. I can't judge too harshly, though, because such verbs as *institutionalize* and *hospitalize* are so entrenched in the language that we roll right over their length without wondering why, for instance, "to hospital" someone never took root. It is, however, acceptable to jail someone.

But I'm not one of those purists who believe slang and invented words ruin our noble tongue. To believe that, I'd have to be willing not to doomscroll or freecycle.

"The pope is poping beautifully," texted my friend Vidya, a journalist, soon after the election of Pope Leo XIV. I find her construction enchanting. Innovation is essential; it keeps the language alive.

Some of my fellow wordsmiths dislike *text* and *google* as verbs. They prefer "send a text" and "search on Google," and I understand. On the other hand, they don't mind verbs such as *format*, to arrange into a computer format, or *yo-yo*, to fluctuate (derived from a trademark). The linguistic process raises questions about language and market dominance, as I'll touch on soon regarding Uber (a verb) and Lyft (not). But creating verbs from brand names and computer and digital terms has historic roots and is here to stay.

I endorse new verbs, with a caveat. I welcome those that catch fire, and the spontaneous one-offs, too, *as long as their meaning is clear.*

Linguists call this age-old process of turning nouns into verbs "denominalizing," that is, making a noun a not-noun. I prefer to call it verbing.

Everybody verbs. Shakespeare emptied his inkwell on scores of innovative verbs, including the wicked, wonderful "*to lip* a wanton on a secure couch." In *Othello*, Iago utters this phrase to ignite Othello's suspicions that his lieutenant is seducing his wife, using a terse, fresh verb burning with carnal heat. F. Scott Fitzgerald, in a letter to the wife of his publisher, conjugated *cocktail* as a verb, including such witty interrogatives as *Cocktailest thou? Dost cocktail? Wilt cocktail?* But the notorious imbiber didn't invent the verb. Its use dates to the 1860s.

The secret to verbing is to ground your new verbs in common knowledge. Listeners and readers need to grasp the meaning on the basis of the new verb itself, the context, and what they know. Verbing is like telling a good joke, and requires instant understanding to work. Explaining kills it.

Drag queen Monét X Change called her one-woman show *Life Be Lifin'*, a title so witty, sharp, and raw it led me to buy a ticket. (I was already a fan but I do like a good title.) The show lived up to its name.

Monét steered us through her Brooklyn beginnings as a queer Black boy to her fame on *RuPaul's Drag Race*, and between the laughs she wove stories of bullying and intimacies, vulnerability and pain, leading right up to now because, as you and I know, life be lifin' *hard* these days. It whipsaws from bonkers to chaos. Any given day might shower us with outrage, anxieties, frustrations, and other blows because, on the whole, life comes down to how we get along. And people be peopling.

I'm going to bet that "life be lifin'" and "people be peopling" make sense even if you haven't encountered the expressions before. Still, let's pause here for a little linguistics and grammar. "Life be lifin'" uses what linguists call the "habitual *be*" or "invariant *be*"; it's a characteristic of African American English and certain regional varieties of English. Habitual *be* indicates actions that are ongoing, or it marks a quality that's embodied, as in "She be smart." Life be lifin' is another (and, let's be honest, cooler) way to say life *is lifing*, where the verbs *to be* and *to life* create what's known as the present continuous tense, which describes continuous action.

In a similar way, I could say life is happening (*to be* + *to happen*). I could say people are being human (*to be* + *to be*) and they're also being capricious and so much more (or less, depending on the day). But sometimes—almost always—I want instant impact, so the blunt, attention-getting option appeals to me. Especially when it sounds relaxed and unaffected.

Invent verbs at will, but make sure they're clear to others rather than puzzling.

Here, as everywhere in writing, grace and clarity are key. "Verbing weirds language," as Calvin said to Hobbes. The goal is not to weird one's words. The goal is perfect pitch.

* * *

COME NERD OUT OVER OUR NEW MIX-INS! urges the pole sign outside an ice cream shop near my house. Forget the mix-ins, big guy—I'm nerding out over the language. That irresistible invitation combines nominalizing ("mix-in": verb becomes noun) and denominalizing ("nerd out": noun as part of a verb).

Just about any noun has the potential to become a verb. But for a new verb to take off, it must pass the kitchen-table test: Will average folks get the new verb if they've never heard it before?

Examples from the kitchen table: We can fork over cash, spoon with our soulmate, knife through waves in a speedboat, butter up the boss, liquor up the in-laws, and get juiced for a party.

A literal meaning may lie inside the verb—the phrasal verb *fork over*, meaning to give away something on demand, likely emerged from the act of serving food on a fork to someone. But even if one can argue that there's a literal, logical meaning lurking inside one's newly coined verb, that's no guarantee it will come into fashion.

Let's look at some other kitchen-adjacent words and see what happens when they're denominalized: Napkin up a mistake? Casserole the assets and filet the options? These are cumbersome. Too much mental squinting goes into figuring out the meaning.

I made up those examples, but here's one I read in a novel recently that stopped me: "Her arms wheelbarrowed." The author was describing someone dancing. Does *wheelbarrowed* make sense to you? I don't get a clear picture from it. If the author had written, "Her arms windmilled," I'd understand a large, circling, whipping force.

In a comprehensive 1979 study, Stanford University linguists Eve V. Clark and Herbert H. Clark investigated the pragmatics of creating verbs from nouns, which they argued is an intrinsic part of our capacity to use language. People invent them to economize; these innovative denominal verbs cut back on words, space, and time by expressing a lengthy concept in an instant. Given the right context, such newly invented words can hit home if—this is crucial—we share common experiences. The Clarks stress that interpreting them depends on context, and mutual knowledge is essential.

Take this sentence: When Steve left Emily, he thought she'd fall to pieces, but Emily had therapized for that.

Everything coming before *therapized* establishes that the sentence is about a bad breakup. *Therapized* fits into that context.

Emily, by the way, is fine. She skipped off and Harleyed the hell out of the Blue Ridge Parkway.

Likewise, in a column headlined "The Memeing of Life," *GQ* can be confident that readers will understand this assertion: "In fact, for a political idea to connect, it very much has to meme." (Editor Will Welch, who wrote the column, helps fill out *meme* as a verb by referring to "a deliriously craven lust for LOLs.")

Reporters like to play with the language they sling around every day, so we often find innovative denominal verbs in journalism. As one linguist explained to me, journalists possess language antennae tuned to fresh usage, contemporary culture, and any new words that their sources bandy about. Reporters don't usually flinch at bending and extending the rules of language, adding a suffix or a verb ending, and creating a neologism.

I've dabbled in this myself. In a story about the high technical demands of ballroom dance competitions, I wrote that getting wildly creative at the expense of technique "is not what's going to grand-slam those titles." In an interview of Kevin Costner, I noted that his movie *Open Range* looked like "an attempt to giddyap a career." Did I invent those verbs? Doubtful. It's likely they were swirling in the ether, and my subconscious, long before.

However, I plant my flag on one particular verb. It sprang to mind some years ago, when the choreographer Merce Cunningham—eighty-four at the time, and the venerable guru of avante-garde dance—collaborated on a new dance with two hot, adventurous rock bands. Deafening buzz ensued. Tickets to the premiere sold out months in advance. The dance's title, *Split Sides*, evoked the fever and the fear. Might a mosh pit emerge? *Was the world ready for this mind-bending rock ballet?* I set the scene in verbs:

> Despite the loud, wailing and sometimes quite lovely contributions of alternative rock bands Radiohead and Sigur Rós, the Merce Cunningham Dance Company didn't really rock, and it didn't really roll. Gurgled and boinged and yeeeeeearrr-roooOWWWed was more like it.

The outpourings of a soundboard take on even more force when you verb them.

Verbing isn't limited to nouns, however. A preposition can become a verb, too. To *at* someone—to tag on social media, using the @ sign with their username—can lead to the colossal loss of time and dignity known as an internet fight. This is why "atting" is often expressed as a plea in the negative, because the writer doesn't want to tangle with X/Twittersphere: *Duke's is the best mayo don't @ me.*

Like writing, coining words can be a creative thrill, and anyone can do it. Humans have been making up words since utterances first flew out of their mouths. Language change is normal and continuous, and denominal verbs aren't corruptions. They're signs of agility and imagination. They stock our collective lexicon with new terms fished from the waters we swim in, waters that wash us with new information every day.

The American Dialect Society celebrates new words and takes an irreverent approach to its Word of the Year elections. In 2024, for instance, the society's members—linguists, lexicographers, etymologists, grammarians, and other wordsmiths—crowned the verb *rawdog*. The term arose as slang for having sex without a condom, but the meaning soon included doing anything without protecting or preparing yourself. As the ADS website notes, "*rawdogging* ended up crossing over into mainstream usage for a wide variety of activities, like the travel trend in which a passenger sits through a flight without any distractions."

Rawdog follows the ADS's 2023 winner: *enshittification.* (I'm not a fan of *-ation* verbal nouns, as you know from chapter 2, but this one is clever. I envision a verb: *enshittify.*) The word's popularity spiked after Cory Doctorow, an author and journalist (naturally), used the word in a blog post: "Here is how platforms die," he wrote. "First, they are good to their users; then they abuse their users to make things better for their business customers; finally, they abuse those business customers to claw back all the value for themselves. Then, they die. I call this enshittification."

Sounds right.

* * *

Yet an age-old prejudice exists against new verbs, one you may have heard, and it goes like this: Back in my day we knew where we stood with verbs and they were Latin and stately and nowadays verbs are ridiculous jumbles.

I don't buy it, though I do appreciate the wish for strength and dignity in language.

For instance, I'm wary of *demagogue* as a verb, as in "Rather than address the issues at the convention, he demagogued the crowd." For one thing, the word is cumbersome; for another, it's vague. It's a complicated noun—*Merriam-Webster* defines it as "a leader who makes use of popular prejudices and false claims and promises in order to gain power"—and that makes the transition to verbhood difficult. It schmears over things. What are the specific actions?

Diligence as a verb also sounds suspicious to me. As shorthand for the process of exercising due diligence, it reduces the actions of attention and analysis to jargon. From an investment company's website: "To date the firm has sourced, structured, diligenced, funded and serviced more than $1.5 billion in financing . . ." The whole statement sounds like funky weirdspeak.

But it's worth remembering that the very large number of denominal verbs we use routinely—the Clarks listed more than thirteen hundred in their study—were once new constructions. A few examples: diaper a baby, fence a yard, hem pants, label boxes, moonlight as a tutor, nail a door shut, spice the stew. And on and on.

The verb *boycott* comes from a person's name. In 1880, Irish activists organized a protest against Captain Charles C. Boycott, a British land agent in Ireland. They urged his employees to stop working and the local community to shun him. Boycott became such a popular verb that, as the *Oxford English Dictionary* notes, the French rushed to adopt it (with *boycotter*), and other European languages followed: German *boycottieren* (now *boykottieren*), Dutch *boycotten*, Russian *boykotirovat*, and more. *Girlcott* followed in 1884.

Think of the famous names to use with dramatic effect today: Let's Churchill this problem. He just couldn't Jagger his energy.

New areas of technology give rise to denominal verbs—many of them phrasal verbs, with prepositions attached—because there's no better way to describe the function. Thus we log in, scroll down, upload, and download. Digital natives circulate catchy, useful innovative verbs, especially in the realm of online behaviors and related phenomena. We're all emailing, DMing, and WhatsApping, reflecting our collective enmeshment with technology. My son told me that when he set out from Pittsburgh to slice through the Appalachians on his bike, he wound up Google Mapsing his way to the trail. On the way to finding travel shortcuts, he made a linguistic one, in this case a gerund. Adventurers are more inclined to DIY their expeditions than to trip-stack them, pandemic style, with layers of backup plans.

To Instagram a photo or Venmo money: These verbs spring from the deep-rooted habit of creating verbs from category-killing brand names.

People who videotaped, back in the day, or who bubble-wrap breakables, superglue a shoe, FedEx a package, or hoover up hot dogs are using brand-name verbs. (Along with the recognizable FedEx, Super Glue Corporation, and Hoover vacuum cleaners, there's Sealed Air Corporation—inventors of Bubble Wrap—and the Ampex Corporation—owners of the original *videotape* trademark.)

When people say they're Ubering somewhere—even if they're riding in a Lyft—Uber blows a kiss. Achieving verb status is a mark of distinction for a brand name; it has lodged in people's minds as *the* defining experience of a thing. Is "Let's Waymo there" far off? That company, which operates robotaxis and a ride-sharing service, warns on its website against using its trademark as a verb. But the public decides what clicks. And according to an article in *Forbes*, the new orthodoxy for brand managers is "control verbs, not nouns."

Perhaps this is because nouns are static and verbs, of course, aren't, and action may be the more appealing corporate characteristic. This makes sense for action-oriented brands such as transportation and search services. Attaining verbhood isn't easy, however. It usually requires inventing a new category of service and flooding the market with ads. A simple, catchy name that can't be confused with an existing verb helps. (This may be part of the problem for Lyft.)

But for the company that gets it right? "You will likely be rewarded," says *Forbes*, "by owning that verb for the rest of time." An optimistic view, and not always the case. Xerox, for example, appeared as a verb in the 1960s. It still surfaces nowadays, but we're apt to use *copy* instead.

Denominal verbs and other neologisms pour forth so quickly that formal language references have elaborate procedures to track their usage. *Merriam-Webster* began citation files back in the 1880s to keep pace with new words, tracking them until they're in widespread use across a range of publications. At that point the dictionary may enshrine them.

This can take time. *Stan*, for example, came into *Merriam-Webster*'s online dictionary in 2019 after first emerging in the 2000 song "Stan" by rapper Eminem. The song depicts a crazed, obsessed fan. Stan was first a noun but the verb arose soon enough, meaning "to exhibit fandom to an extreme or excessive degree; to be an extremely devoted and enthusiastic fan of someone or something." To wit: *Stanning BTS*, the name of a podcast—and a gerund phrase—that serves BTS's ultra-dedicated ARMY, as stans of the Korean boy band are known.

Emoji-verbs are sure to follow into formal reference works, as in this headline: "I ♥ a Hate-Watch. Don't You?"

Chillax is in *Merriam-Webster*, but *cry-laugh* is not. (Neither is *laugh-cry*.) That doesn't mean we can't use it, because we definitely do it. Especially when we're hate-watching (which *is* in there). In my case that means putting myself through *Dateline: Secrets Uncovered.*

I realize the series has lasted for years and has many sincere and devoted fans (stans?). But as you and I know, part of the ♥ of hate-watching is that it's a bit subversive. Yes, it's high time for some slick, voyeuristic melodrama whose promises hook me and irk me every time, while chillaxing with the cat and thinking of grander things. Like where I'll summer.

* * *

The background and meanings of many innovative verbs are clear enough. But as for who, in particular, invented them and made them popular? Now the plot thickens.

Dante, Chaucer, Shakespeare, and other literary masters picked up on the vernacular of their day and spread it through their writing; this we know. But linguists caution against crediting the big names with *inventing* words from scratch. We can't travel back in time, and we don't have recordings of vernacular speech from hundreds of years ago. Written works are the only record of language from centuries past.

Shakespeare is said to have invented nearly two thousand words, though it's likely he heard them first in the streets of London or Stratford-upon-Avon, or—also likely—from his wife, her girlfriends, and other young folk.

We can only extrapolate from contemporary language research. And that research tells a strong story: Women drive the innovation.

"Cigarette me, big boy," purred the young actor and dancer Ginger Rogers, flicking her fat fur collar off her little bare shoulder in the 1930 film *Young Man of Manhattan*. She got what she wanted (the cigarette, the man), and soon everyone in the 1930s was bumming smokes with her line. She followed the golden rule: clarity above all. And her meaning was clear, wasn't it? Where there's smoking, there's flirting and maybe more. Instant messaging!

I raise this example because I'm going to turn down a new path here. I want to dig a little deeper into biases and judgment about new verbs. The ire over new verbs, when you hear it, is often aimed at young people, chiefly at young women.

Whether through a clever script or her own embellishment, Ginger Rogers led a sisterhood of smokers in a historical pattern that linguists know well. Women—especially young women—have the greatest ability to spread new words. Why? Linguists point to innate early language abilities combined with girls' general empathetic awareness. Their social networks tend to be larger than boys', which exposes girls and young women to diverse language influences.

Sali A. Tagliamonte, head of linguistics at the University of Toronto, specializes in the speech of adolescents and young adults. "Young women are on the front lines of linguistic change," she told me. "They are inherently good linguistically. They tend to develop vocabulary faster than boys. It's a biological thing, not one hundred percent of course, but the tendency is there. And the culture propagates that. Women are more able to use their own societies for using language. Men have their strength, their wit, their bro culture. Women have a different modus operandi."

Tagliamonte finds that girls and young women gravitate to what's fresh, cool, and fashionable in words as well as in clothes, music, and the like. They're generally more open to taking creative leaps with language than their male counterparts, who may wait until a word is widely accepted to use it. Young men "tend to deviate less from each other, and women tend to want to stand out," Tagliamonte said. "Women use language as a commodity, in a way."

Certainly words are marvelous tools to discover, play with, flaunt, and share. And of all the things commodified across social media, a vintage verb coming into vogue is something to cheer. That's what happened when the young actor and singer Kira Kosarin created a TikTok video a couple years ago about a Scottish verb from the early 1800s: *hurkle-durkle*. She served forth a term for lazing around in bed that had largely fallen out of use. Until it went viral.

Hurkle-durkle spread through social media the way "Cigarette me, big boy" seeped into common speech. The well-known British lexicographer Susie Dent had helped spread the old Scots verb back in 2016 by announcing it on Twitter (now X): "Hurkle-durkle: a 200 year-old Scottish term meaning to lounge in bed long after it's time to get up." She added: "Happiness is hurkle-durkling."

Dent has a wonderful title: She is the resident lexicographer of a long-running British game show that involves word and math tasks, and she has a healthy social media following. Legions of grateful hurkle-durklers shared her post over the years. Dent reposted it from time to time, and in early 2024 Kosarin took note. The twenty-something star of Nickelodeon's *The Thundermans* devotes frequent TikToks to offbeat words and phrases, and her droll homage to hurkle-durkling caught fire.

"I do be hurkling and I do be durkling," Kosarin confesses in the video, narrowing her eyes to make clear she takes her layabouts seriously. "And once I've hurkled my last durkle in a given morning I will get up. But I'm a big fan of a hurkle-durkle. So you should be, too."

Four million views later, #hurkledurkle had flooded TikTok and countless other hurkle-durkle tribute videos popped up.

Who knew we were a nation, nay, a world, of rebellious alarm-clock-triggered burnouts? On second thought, it makes complete sense—hello, post-pandemic change fatigue—and the better question is, why did we ever let such a charming verb for this universal behavior die off?

One TikTok commenter spoke to that: "I'm going to use 'hurkle durkle' instead of 'bed rot' from now on."

* * *

Biases invariably pop up when we start talking about language change. In the 1970s and '80s people blamed an emerging "and, like, you know, I was in the car?" pattern of speech on a lingo invasion by rich white schoolgirls in California's San Fernando Valley. Every sentence swept upward into a question, proof, the thinking went, of the girls' core uncertainty and ditziness.

Yet linguistic studies found that the "uptalk" lilt cut across ethnicity, socioeconomic class, and gender. It was widely dispersed in Southern California beyond the Valley. In fact, it exists throughout the English-speaking world, and it predated the 1970s. Valley girl speech was a myth. The uptalk shift may have been gaining momentum among young people in SoCal; girls were likely more attuned to the trend, as they usually are, and the broader culture followed.

We all make social judgments about language, misguided and otherwise. Is "life be lifin'" clever, creative, improper, or, used by those outside the Black community, appropriation? What about "I do be hurkling?" How we hear it, and how we view the speaker, depends on a personal, complicated interplay of backgrounds, bias, and, yes, age.

Young people, young women especially, tend to draw blame in kerfuffles over new words. But by spreading contemporary terms and phrasing, youthful stylists join wordsmiths of the past in a timeless game: extending the rules of language.

"The tendency is for teenagers to push the changes forward—not that they create them, but they up the ante, push them forward, up until their early twenties or so," Tagliamonte said. "And young women push things a bit more. But the truth is, nobody invents language, really. They just push forward little developments."

Adding a verb ending to a noun, making nouns from verbs, playing with words. Changes in how we use language, whether large or small, can raise alarm, but that's nothing new. Around twenty-five hundred years ago, Socrates worried that oral recitation was dying out, and that would lead to terrible things. Memory and wisdom, the great philosopher feared, were goners.

What did he blame for this dangerous attack on intelligence?

Writing.

* * *

Good Habits

- In his poem "The Bull," Ocean Vuong writes, "He stood alone in the backyard, so dark / the night purpled around him." In *Mrs Dalloway*, Virginia Woolf refers to "blackberrying in the sun." Writers have always played with verbing to create fresh, potent effects. Write a paragraph or two that includes at least five of your own verbed verbs. Be creative. (Picasso it!) Make up verbs or draw on what you hear from friends, on social media, in song lyrics and poems—anywhere people play with words.

- Add a verbing section to your metaphor lists from the end of chapter 8. Jot down ones you come across in movies, podcasts, or articles. Use them to inspire your own when you want to add attitude and verve.

  From my own notes on the Jason Statham movie *The Beekeeper*: "I gotta big-dog this" and "You can't come up here white-knighting [stuff]." Plenty of bee puns, too.

CHAPTER 10

Stimulate

This is your brain on verbs: the surprising science behind their power to move minds and bodies.

> Writing is perhaps the greatest of human inventions, binding together people, citizens of distant epochs, who never knew one another.
>
> —CARL SAGAN

Hit

What does it feel like to read that word? What do you picture?

Smash

How is that different?

The distinction proved crucial in an experiment by Elizabeth Loftus, a psychology professor at the University of California, Irvine. Loftus is a leading expert in memory—the fallibility of memory, to be exact. Much of her research focuses on wording. She studies how asking people questions using one verb or another influences what they remember. What she found suggests the great power that verbs wield to shape our memories and imagination.

This chapter is quite different from the others, which addressed the more prescriptive ideas about verbs and how to use them. Here, I want to think about how verbs affect our minds and bodies.

Loftus's work is a good place to start. In one experiment, she asked people to watch police films of car accidents and answer written questions about what they had seen. One group read this question: How fast were the cars going when they hit each other?

Another group read: How fast were the cars going when they smashed together?

Loftus discovered that the phrases "hit each other" and "smashed together" prompted different answers about speed. The people who read "How fast were the cars going when they smashed together?" estimated the cars were traveling 5 to 10 mph faster than those asked about cars hitting each other. People who read about cars smashing together were also more likely to report seeing broken glass—though there was no broken glass in the film.

We know that in terms of their definitions, *smash* tells a different, more violent story than *hit*. But Loftus's work shows us, empirically, *how* different: Her experiment demonstrated how a written verb can shape what a reader has *already seen*. Reading *smash* sways the entire event and leaves its mark on memory, transforming how people remembered a wreck they had just seen.

This is just one experiment that presented language to people and measured what happens. Scientists have made many other discoveries, especially in the field of cognitive science, which focuses on the mind and intelligence. What emerges from this work is a scientific basis for why the specificity of verbs, and making choices among verbs, matters, from biological and physiological standpoints. Compelling new findings have a great deal to tell us about the psychological and emotional power of verbs.

Here's an example. We're familiar with motion metaphors such as "Her love of music carried her through her recovery" or my mother's favorite, "Have you done your homework yet? Hop to it." Cognitive scientist Teenie Matlock is interested in how people interpret a specific kind of motion metaphor, called "nonliteral motion metaphors." These involve inanimate objects in expressions such as "The road runs along the coast" and "The trail goes north from here." Matlock has used such cognitive measures as reading times to investigate how people make sense of this kind of language. Her early studies looked at how long people took to read the sentence "The road runs along the coast." Would the time vary across contexts, for instance, while thinking about a rugged terrain versus a smooth one?

And how might people process a sentence such as "The road meanders along the coast"? Would they process any of these statements in a way that reflects actual motion?

I called Matlock, who is professor emerita at the University of California, Merced, to talk about her results. She told me that when we read about something meandering, the brain recognizes that the verb describes a slow action, and it simulates the verb's serpentine motion in a slow way. Measurements of participants' reading times and eye movements suggest slower processing, something the brain does even when the object meandering is inanimate, like a road. Matlock terms this fictive motion. No earthquakes or Marvel characters are shaking up the asphalt; no animated Tour de France–style video is showing an incrementally moving route. The road is fixed.

"Our brains are wired to simulate motion," Matlock told me. "And when we're using language either as a speaker or listener, we're predisposed to simulate actions we're talking about or reading about."

This is even more evident, she said, in sentences like "A cord runs along the wall," where the object in "motion" has no association with motion (unlike roads and trails). Still, reading about its figurative, fictive motion triggers a fleeting sense of movement in the reader's unconscious mind.

Matlock cautions that this simulating is not the same as the conscious use of one's full-blown imagination to picture something in detail. But it demonstrates that our verb choices can move our readers before they're even aware of it. "The road meanders" takes the reader's mind on a journey. The verb conveys meaning that the unconscious mind absorbs and follows, leading it to meander along with the writer's intention. So when we choose a verb, we're communicating tempo and tone.

Imagine writing a travel blog or website copy about the Scottish coast, or crafting a fictional scene set near Singapore's port. Might any given passage be a moment for quick action, or for a leisurely, winding one? A time to speed your audience along or slow it down?

* * *

As readers, we test language's effect on us with every word. Take, for example, Edgar Allan Poe's story "The Tell-Tale Heart." The excerpt below comes just after the narrator has murdered an old man, cut up the body, and stashed it under the floorboards. The police arrive and the murderer plays it cool, welcoming them into the very room where he has buried his victim. But as the police start questioning him, a noise fills his ears, surely the old man's heartbeat.

> Why would they not be gone? I paced the floor to and fro with heavy strides, as if excited to fury by the observations of the men—but the noise steadily increased. Oh God! what could I do? I foamed—I raved—I swore! I swung the chair upon which I had been sitting, and grated it upon the boards, but the noise arose over all and continually increased. It grew louder—louder—louder! And still the men chatted pleasantly, and smiled. Was it possible they heard not? Almighty God!—no, no! They heard!—they suspected!—they knew!—they were making a mockery of my horror!

Did your breathing change, even slightly, while reading it? Did your breath catch, slow, or quicken? Maybe the *whoosh* of a chair arcing through space flashed in your mind. Perhaps you felt a slight pressing in your ears, as if those loud noises were nearby. To be sure, your experience may be different from mine, as we all react in our own ways. Nevertheless, scientists who embrace a concept known as "embodied cognition" believe that we're all subtly activating our motor and perceptual systems when we use language.

Broadly speaking, embodied cognition proposes that our behavior and understanding arise from our nervous system, body, and environment, and the interconnections of all three, rather than from computations in the brain alone. According to the embodied cognition theory, the mind is a full-body system.

So when it comes to reading, the words seem to spark representations in our brains that involve the sensorimotor systems of our bodies. The representations may be images of a sort, or flickers of feeling, which spring from our life experiences and the sensory information surrounding them.

Say I'm describing a passing car, and I write, "The car whizzes past"—did you feel something? That kind of verb, implying speed and carrying its own sound effect, may trigger a little sensation, a slight feeling or a sound.

I'd been tapping into this in my writing before I learned about the research, and perhaps you have, too. One of my chief goals as a critic is to immerse readers in what I'm seeing and stir their own feelings about it. Then, I hope, readers will inhabit the scene vicariously, whether it's a flamenco performance I feel in my bones or, in a feature story I wrote several years ago, my view from a catwalk high above a stadium floor. I had climbed up there to watch upriggers hang lights for a Jennifer Lopez concert.

For that story, I didn't want to sketch how the concert setup happens, with who does what and why. I wanted to know what it *felt like* to stagger onto that swinging bridge over nothingness, and I wanted to bring readers up there with me. So I wrote about starting to pant as the abyss pressed in. And how one of the riggers—so cheerful and carefree though it was 7 a.m. and he was working a hundred feet in the air—calmed my hyperventilating. He did it just by strolling past me on the catwalk "as if he were ambling down the street on the happiest day of his life, the harness forcing his legs wide so that he bounced and rolled a bit from side to side." Reading that, you may have visualized those actions, and felt a hint of a jiggle, too.

This process happens automatically, scientists believe, and largely without our conscious awareness.

This seems to play out in the experiments we've just read about. Given similar verbs with nuanced shades of meaning, such as *run* and *meander*, or *smash* and *hit*, people's cognitive unconscious understands them quite differently—and research suggests this comes down to how the verbs stir memories and resonate internally.

It makes sense that our bodies and physical experiences shape our understanding. Poe, a writer with extraordinary dramatic powers and command of figurative language, knew this intuitively. In the excerpt from "The Tell-Tale Heart," visceral verbs describe whiplashing emotions. The noise itself behaves like a monster; it "arose over all and continually increased." Strong, clear action, exclamation points all over: This scene is a serenity killer. It's not for someone seeking to wind down.

Great writing thrills us with its power to move us in surprising ways. As the French essayist and literary critic Roland Barthes wrote, "The pleasure of the text is that moment when my body pursues its own ideas."

But if Martians peered into our nervous systems while we read Poe's thrillers or any other dramatic work, they'd surely be amazed that little black marks on a page, or particles on a screen, can unleash a flood of physical reactions over which we have no control.

* * *

Language is magical—how else to describe it? We have this fragile, squishy, silent brain locked up in our skull, but through language we free it to connect with its fellows. Language allows us to mesh our minds, to hijack other people's thoughts for a moment and persuade them to think *our* thoughts, to know *our* desires and ideas.

We are inherently social animals, but how would we get to know one another without language? It gives us new perspectives and stories that make us think differently about our own. And yet, though language is basic to every human society on the planet, scientists don't understand everything about how it works and how we make meaning from words.

Until recently, it wasn't possible to see inside a brain and watch it think. It's not even easy to think about thinking without thinking itself getting in the way. Nevertheless, hypotheses abound.

New research on embodied cognition suggests something exciting for writers: that paying attention to verbs, and using dynamic verbs when appropriate, is more than a matter of style and craft. Vivid verbs aren't just a way to flex vocabulary. There's neural function behind their power.

First, let's think about your brain and its tens of billions of neurons for a moment—but bear in mind, thinking is perhaps the *least* of their many concerns. Your brain's number one job is looking out for Number One, and much of this involves planning and executing movement. The brain's motor system enables us to move through life with our evolutionary goals: to find food and eat it, to avoid *getting* eaten and other bad things, and to create relationships and keep them.

Here's where embodied cognition comes in. In the 1970s linguists such as George Lakoff at the University of California, Berkeley, helped shape the field of cognitive linguistics. This field seeks to align the study of language with what's known about cognition from other related fields, in disciplines such as neuroscience, psychology, philosophy, and artificial intelligence. Applying such sciences to linguistics, Lakoff and others came to believe that inside our heads, when we read, we engage our "motor program," as well as mental images, to make meaning. We rely on how our bodies, and our embodied brains, interact with the world.

Scientists can watch people make meaning from words in real time. They use fMRI scanners (which track blood flow to the brain areas working hardest) for this, as well as high-speed cameras that track eye movements, and sweat-detecting fingertip sensors. From their observations, a hypothesis of embodied simulation emerged: We mentally simulate what the experiences expressed in language feel like.

Benjamin K. Bergen, a cognitive scientist at the University of California, San Diego, has studied embodied simulation extensively and has written a fascinating book about it, *Louder Than Words: The New Science of How the Mind Makes Meaning.* He told me that language is so intricate and complex, it excites the entire brain.

"We know that as people are processing language or producing language, there is activation across the brain, not just in language areas," he said. "It's a whole-brain process."

Much of this process involves motor areas. Bergen brings up a surprising example that suggests just how much we rely on simulating motion to understand words. In some cases, people with lesions in their motor cortex—the brain area involved in moving our skeletal muscles—can't name pictures of certain things, such as a hammer or a cat. However, they can name pictures of a skyscraper or a giraffe.

Why is this?

One hypothesis for the picture-naming struggle is that lesions in the motor cortex may disrupt certain motor simulations, and cats and hammers lose their meaning. Let's think about what we do with a hammer. We dig it out of the toolbox, pick it up, and carry it. We interact with it physically. Same with cats: We stroke them, lift them off the keyboard. Our understanding of "cat" and "hammer" is enmeshed with our hands, arms, and muscles—with our motor system.

But most of us will never get close enough to a giraffe to touch it. A skyscraper is also far removed; it's something we gaze up at, see from a distance. Giraffes and skyscrapers are more likely to trigger visual images in the brain, not motor ones.

So much for nouns. What about verbs? Bergen says that verbs tend to activate the motor parts of the brain, from the primary motor cortex through other premotor and supplemental motor areas, "selectively, by body part."

What does this mean? The primary motor cortex is a strip of brain tissue in the frontal lobe, and different areas of it control different parts of the body. When people slide into an fMRI machine and they hear the verbs *pick* or *lick*, their brains show activity in the areas that send messages to the muscles of the hands or mouth. Bergen described another experiment that tracked how fast people pressed buttons, and phrases such as "grabbing the keys" from someone triggered faster reactions than "handing the keys" to someone. In general, he said, action language "drives a re-creation in the brain of the actions being described."

He's also seen this with metaphorical action language. "With any motion that's represented as bodily motion, such as 'The economy is crawling back from the abyss,' we know that the brain lights up in motor-specific ways in response to those verbs," Bergen said. This includes hand-moving areas (these, he said, get excited when a person reads, "You've got to hand it to him, he knows what he's doing") or mouth-moving areas (activated by, for example, "That's too ridiculous for me to swallow").

But Bergen points out an interesting wrinkle. The extent to which metaphorical language trips our brains' motor areas depends on how unconventional the metaphor is.

"Some are so familiar we don't even notice them," Bergen said. So hearing "We've just kicked off our campaign" is unlikely to spark much motor simulation. But what about "That idea is difficult, so I'm going to have to gargle on it for a while"?

"That's an unusual use of the verb," Bergen said, "so you're going to simulate what it's like to gargle and then transfer some inferences. Versus 'I see what you mean,' which is mostly a shortcut."

Bergen's research shows that even abstract language has an effect on the physical body, and the physical body—the one that crawls back, jumps in with both feet, and gargles—gives us abstract language. Then our brains turn *that* around and say, honey, that's a *motor* image, you feel me?

It's enough to scramble your brains thinking about it. (Did you just feel a flick of a whisk?)

* * *

While people may unconsciously *feel* what verbs describe, learning to *use* verbs does not come easy. I'm going to take a detour into how children learn verbs, because the process reveals some interesting things about verbs—so transient and invisible—and how they affect us.

In general, children acquire verbs with some difficulty and late in the game. I realized this early one morning when our toddler son woke us with urgent news.

"Big plant!" he exclaimed. He was not yet two and an early riser, prone to roaming.

"Big plant . . . over! Plant over!"

I must have mumbled something unsatisfactory, for the little guy pressed his forehead to mine, eyes wide. He waved behind him, indicating the stairs. "Down dere!"

Still I missed his point. A searching look crossed his face, and after a beat he cried:

"*Fall* over! Big plant fall over!"

Oh!

Finding a verb—and announcing it—made all the difference. I stumbled out of bed knowing just what he meant. The evidence was on the living-room floor, where our tall, trumpet-shaped amaryllis lay in pieces after toppling off the mantel. (The cat. *Of course*, the cat.)

Pity the babies. The English language is so difficult for them with its verbs.

Verbs, let's agree, rule communication. Linguists go so far as to think of sentences as extensions of verbs with other accoutrements. But verbs can be capricious. English has some two hundred irregular ones. And at least for English-speaking children, verbs of any sort are nearly unfathomable for the first couple years of life.

All the forms, functions, flexibility, and nuances that verbs possess make them highly expressive elements of language. Yet unlike nouns, verbs are invisible. They have no shape, weight, or color, and this ephemeral quality makes them the most difficult for small children to master in speech.

So while babies are fascinated by motion—no surprise, given our movement-directed brains—they shy away from verbs, at first. It takes English-speaking children longer to use verbs than other parts of speech. By their first birthday they typically speak a noun or two, and soon they may build their vocabularies by another word or more a week. But verbs aren't likely to appear until later, as the second birthday approaches.

Before then, when little ones want to talk about motion, they use nouns and prepositions. ("Plant over!") Babies learn the broad concepts first: concrete nouns, short directional words such as *up*, *down*, *in*, *out*, and the ever-useful *no*.

This pattern, however, seems to be different among children

learning other languages. San Diego State University linguist Soonja Choi and her colleagues found less of a noun bias in Korean-speaking children, perhaps because Korean parents and caregivers place more emphasis on verbs. Choi's research suggests that children *can* acquire verbs early with encouragement. Her results reveal that Korean caregivers speak to children with more action verbs but fewer object nouns than American caregivers. Korean caregivers engage youngsters in activity-oriented speech significantly more than Americans.

When I called Choi to ask about activity-oriented speech, she told me about one of her experiments that involved a picture book about an elephant. Choi had given it to American and Korean mothers so they could talk about it with their toddlers.

"American mothers, most of the time, said, 'What is that? It's an elephant,'" she said. "But Korean mothers said, 'What is it *doing*? What is the elephant doing?' They were eliciting verbs versus eliciting nouns."

"It's not that children are cognitively only able to process entities," Choi said. "They can process events and the change of events." She found that by the time Korean-speaking children have learned fifty to eighty words, 25 percent of them are verbs, while for English-speaking children, 10 percent are verbs.

Word order may also play a part in how quickly children learn verbs, Choi said. English, with its subject-verb-object structure, has what linguists call a verb-second order; verbs are in the second position. But Korean, like Japanese, Turkish, and many Native American languages, is verb final—its sentences generally *end* in verbs. "So instead of 'I take an apple,'" Choi told me, "Koreans say 'I apple take.'"

"This highlights the verb in language acquisition," she said. "Children pay attention to the last word in discourse because it remains in memory more than what comes before."

Children learning any language are right to take their time with the complexities of verbs, to mull them over and choose them with care. It's easy to imagine how overwhelming the ins and outs of action language can be when babies are just starting to understand the looming elements of life like pets and trucks and why every day can't be a Cheerios-for-dinner day.

Indeed, verbs can overwhelm no matter the age. For instance, you might not want to listen to a high-action audiobook while you're driving. It's also best, if you're at the wheel, to avoid an evocative podcast that whips up visions of trekking through New Zealand on horseback, say, or swanning around in eighteenth-century finery. Why? Giving the brain too much overlapping action imagery can interfere with processing the action right in front of you, on the road. The act of driving is already putting demands on the brain's motor real estate.

Benjamin Bergen, the cognitive scientist who studies the brain's response to action language, has tested this with driving simulators in his lab. "The idea is if you overwhelm the brain with some kind of language having to do with action, that would interfere with processing action at the same time," he told me.

He was curious about what would happen when people use language that's vision- or motor-specific as they're trying to drive. For example, talking to someone on the phone about where in the store they'll have to look to find the brush they want, and mentally following a path through the aisles while also navigating road traffic.

"We put them in a scenario where they're following a car," Bergen said, "and the motor and visual language they were using interfered with their ability to do that. They responded less quickly."

So you see, it's not just you and it's not just me. Multitasking is a lie.

* * *

The phenomenon of simulation that underpins these studies about verbs, action language, and the brain is compelling. It helps explain why reading a story can feel almost as real as living it. Scores of scientific studies show that reading can activate the same areas of the brain as real life does—those involved with motion, emotions, color sensing, and other senses. I don't need science to tell me this, though.

Here's what I've experienced repeatedly, and I'll bet you have, too. I'll use James Baldwin's *Go Tell It on the Mountain* as an example because the writing stirs up so many associations and it's especially vivid in my mind. The novel is set in a Black fundamentalist community in Harlem during the 1930s. Many of the circumstances in the life of John Grimes, the teenage protagonist, are exceedingly different from my own, yet like John I have yearned, despaired, and doubted, and at one point I was also fourteen. And so when I start reading this book, I'm plunging into waters that feel bracing and fresh but emotionally familiar, and the lightning clarity and energy of Baldwin's prose sets the hook. Before long I'm captive to the story, and when I come to the scene where John falls before the Holy Ghost—to name just one instance—he pulls me into the mystery with him. The description fuels my own surprise, disorientation, and sense of shattering:

> He was invaded, set at naught, possessed. This power had struck John, in the head or in the heart; and, in a moment, wholly, filling him with an anguish that he could never in his life have imagined, that he surely could not endure, that even now he could not believe, had opened him up; had cracked him open, as wood beneath the axe cracks down the middle, as rocks break up; had ripped him and felled him in a moment, so that John had not felt the wound, but only the agony, had not felt the fall, but only the fear; and lay here, now, helpless, screaming, at the very bottom of darkness.

Filling him with an anguish . . . *had cracked him open* . . . as rocks *break up; had ripped him* and *felled him* . . . Baldwin's verb-loading conveys a sense of overwhelming, brutal power, and drives the emotional force of this passage. I read it and feel a sympathetic pressure in my breastbone. (It's the "cracked him open" part that really gets me.)

"Think about how emotions are expressed in novels and poetry," said Teenie Matlock, the cognitive scientist who studied fictive motion. "Verbs do a lot of the heavy lifting to tap into people's emotions and get them to simulate emotions."

We've seen examples of this in literary excerpts throughout this book, and particularly in the discussion of metaphors in chapter 8. Here's another, a passage from Alan Hollinghurst's magnificent and detailed novel *Our Evenings* that makes clear what Matlock is talking about. The narrator, a middle-aged actor and devoted son, recounts his mother's rash decision, while she was mourning her partner's death, to cut down a stand of trees in her yard:

> It changed everything, and the house itself, when I turned and looked back, was stripped bare of its last little margin of mystery. Mum stood and gazed astonished at what had happened—for the first time in my life, she broke down with me, she turned to me, mouth creased and tears tumbling from her eyes, and allowed me to take charge of her, stoop round her seventy-eight-year-old frame and hold her tight while she shook and gasped with sobbing.

Hollinghurst includes nearly twenty verbs and verb forms, most describing physical, bodily responses that I not only visualize but feel, as if mother and son were standing in front of me. As the currents of shock and breathlessness race from one to the other and back again they touch me, too. By the time I read "shook and gasped with sobbing" I believe this grief almost as if it's my own, and I'm cemented to this woman's story.

The studies I've cited in this chapter give us different ways to think about why this happens, why a story can seize us like a magnet. Some of the ways are subtle. Here's one that's not subtle at all. Matlock has investigated the power of metaphor to turn people's feelings into beliefs and motivation. One study examined how describing wildfires using monster metaphors and monster actions can influence people's tendencies to follow evacuation orders.

Reporters and editors commonly refer to wildfires as monsters in motion. Look at these headlines from the January 2025 fires in California: "Los Angeles Wildfires Devour Thousands of Homes, Death Toll Rises to 10" (Reuters); "Fires Tear Through Los Angeles" (NASA.gov); "Palisades Fire Ravages Malibu Leaving Death and Destruction in Its Wake" (*The Malibu Times*).

Matlock and her coauthors found that people are more willing to evacuate when they read accounts that use aggressive, beast-like verbs—*tearing* through cities and *devouring* homes—than when reports describe wildfires with neutral words, without metaphors, using basic verbs such as *starting* and *burning*. Further, the scientists found that metaphors ramped up people's perceptions of risk. Asked to describe the fires, they gave larger estimates about acres and houses burned and lives lost. Metaphors, driven by dramatic verbs, influenced how people reasoned about the fires.

"It probably taps into old myths about dragons and other fire-related beings," Matlock told me. When people face the unfamiliar, "we use what we know and what will be effective, because language use is intentional. You use things that will capture attention and cause action."

So many questions arise in the fear and uncertainty of a wildfire. What direction is the wind blowing, what is my role as a person, a resident, a neighbor? Public messages are not always timely or clear.

Especially during the early phases of a large fire, Matlock said, it makes sense to blare a sense of urgency.

"It's coherent to use this kind of monster language," she said, "because then the fire can be construed as being dangerous and as having intentions."

This is a useful point for climate reporters to ponder, and other writers engaged with the scope and chaos of climate change. Reporting the full story, especially one this serious, requires more than assembling facts and data and quoting this or that official and witness. It requires finding the images that express the truths emotionally, as victims and witnesses perceive them, and in ways that hit readers—verb-driven images that rush into people's brains and bodies via the speedway of embodied simulation.

Take a look at these excerpts from a 2016 CNN report of a massive fire in Canada:

> The sky in northern Alberta's Fort McMurray resembled a wall of fire and smoke.
>
> In all, some 1,600 structures have been destroyed by the fire, Alberta Premier Rachel Notley said.
>
> Paul Spring said his neighborhood went down in flames.
>
> The thick smoke made it hard to see.

Compare that with author John Vaillant's description of the same fire in *Fire Weather*, his nonfiction book about climate change and infernos:

> Entire neighborhoods burned to their foundations beneath a towering pyrocumulus cloud typically found over erupting

> volcanoes. So huge and energetic was this fire-driven weather system that it generated hurricane-force winds and lightning that ignited still more fires many miles away.... All afternoon, cell phones and dashcams captured citizens cursing, praying, and weeping as they tried to escape a suddenly annihilating world where fists of heat pounded on the windows, the sky rained fire, and the air came alive in roaring flame.

Vaillant's account sweeps forward with dynamic verbs and vivid, verb-driven imagery. Of course, CNN's reporters faced very different circumstances than Vaillant: immediate deadline pressure and the difficulties of newsgathering amid chaos as the disaster was unfolding. They didn't yet know all the details, and the responsible choice was to keep it simple. But the contrast illustrates a useful point: Strong verbs and verb-driven imagery can plunge us imaginatively into a scene and reveal what it *feels* like.

The words most likely to move us are those with heat.

* * *

Grammar—shockingly—was not invented to torture high schoolers or send them into deskbound daydreams. In fact, verb forms—i.e., grammar points—are so crucial to communicating meaning that scientists put them under microscopes to study them.

One of the chief ways Matlock has seen verbs influence people's opinions and emotions is through a verb's *aspect*, which indicates how an action unfolds through time. Aspect tells us whether the action started in the past and is still happening in the present, or if it happened for a while and then stopped. (See chapter 2 for a brief refresher.) In essence, the imperfective aspect—*was* verb + *ing*, as in "The hawk was circling"—conveys an ongoing action. Perfective aspect—verb + *ed*, "The hawk circled"—conveys an action that has ended.

Matlock has found that aspect influences how people understand events, and speakers and writers can color a situation by which aspect they use. For example, people tend to believe more action occurs with imperfective descriptions than with perfective descriptions. In one of her studies, people estimated that more houses were painted after reading "John *was painting* houses last summer" than after reading "John *painted* houses last summer."

In another, she found that when her experiment described a fictitious senator's actions using imperfective aspect—"*was taking* hush money from a prominent constituent"—the participants said they were more confident that he would not be reelected than when his actions were described with perfective aspect—"*took* hush money from a prominent constituent." The imperfective aspect (*was taking*) also resulted in higher dollar estimates in responses about the amount of hush money taken.

Was taking vs. *took*: same misdeed, but a few little words change everything. Think of how small these grammar differences are, yet how potent. We sometimes see them used interchangeably. "Back in 2015 he was taking hush money," one person may report, while another writes, "Back in 2015 he took hush money."

But are they interchangeable? "He was taking" conjures an atmosphere of shady dealings. "He took" implies a definite end before something else happened. Yet I wonder how many writers gloss over these distinctions to meet a deadline or speed ahead with the story.

"When you have someone watch a video of a car accident, and then you say, 'Describe what was happening' versus 'What happened?' you get different responses," Matlock said. "It's very easy to manipulate how someone will respond. Take 'You sneered at me' versus 'You were sneering,' which extends it in time, makes it worse."

* * *

With verbs, the possibilities for nuance and elasticity are endless. As a writer you can sift your imagination, select from the existing storehouse, or invent your own words. You can send your verb through time, extend or shorten its duration, transform it into other parts of speech, tailor it to a context, use it to drive a sentence forward or ease up on the gas—and, most wondrous of all, create a feeling or an idea in another person.

As James Baldwin said, you have to go the way your blood beats. Verbs allow us to write the way our blood beats—and to make our readers' blood beat, too.

* * *

Good Habits

In this chapter we've seen that verbs can manipulate our emotions, which makes our verb choices even more important. To develop a feel for how verbs swing emotions, read news articles and listen to podcasts for instances where the verb twists meaning in an important way.

Here's one example: Many news reports said US gymnast Jordan Chiles "was stripped" of the bronze medal she won at the Paris Olympics. "Stripping" a medal, however, is a punitive action reserved for athletes who've doped or committed other serious violations. In fact, Chiles's conduct was never in question. The dispute involved a purported oversight of the judges and the timing of the US coach's appeal. Judges reversed their decision a couple times and dropped Chiles in the rankings. Yet "stripped" implies much worse associations, lumping the athlete in with cheaters.

A more nuanced example: After a disastrous debate performance, President Biden faced calls to leave the 2024 presidential race. He refused. Former House speaker Nancy Pelosi swept in and gave a headline-making interview. The fallout focused on her use of *decide*: "It's up to the president to decide if he is going to run," she said on MSNBC. "We're all encouraging him to make that decision, because time is running short." Journalists and pundits chewed on the verb. No one thought Pelosi was confused about whether Biden had decided or not. So what did she mean? Was she trying to change the narrative by implying he had only been dithering at that point, not deciding? Or was this an outright call for him to flip his decision and not run?

Note any other instances of canny, unwarranted, or otherwise charged verb use that you come across. Keep them in your notebook. You may find yourself with a topic for an essay, column, or research paper.

CHAPTER 11

Transform

What does it mean to Ulysses Grant your life?

> O world, I cannot hold thee close enough!
> Thy winds, thy wide grey skies!
> Thy mists, that roll and rise!
>
> —EDNA ST. VINCENT MILLAY,
> "GOD'S WORLD"

Shortly before he died of throat and tongue cancer, Ulysses Grant penciled a final note to his doctor.

> I do not sleep though I sometimes doze off a little. If up I am talked to and in my efforts to answer cause pain. The fact is I think I am a verb instead of a personal pronoun. A verb is anything that signifies to be; to do; or to suffer. I signify all three.

Grant, at first blush, seems like an unusual person to craft such a statement—and what a statement. Unforgettable. Plainspoken poetry.

Grant was not a literary person. He wrote to get the job done. The victorious Civil War general wrote his own orders. As president, he wrote his own speeches and other documents. At the very end of his days, he produced—grudgingly, at first—a two-volume memoir. He wrote it solely to earn royalties for his wife, Julia, to live on after he died, because he'd lost his entire wealth to swindlers. As he faced a gruesome terminal disease, possibly the result of a long habit of cigar smoking, all Grant had left was his past—his story. None other than Mark Twain, a close friend, convinced him it would sell.

So Grant gritted his teeth and wrote the book he'd never intended to write. To be sure, surrendering was not his way. He was still working on the last volume when he sent that note about being a verb to his doctor. Just days after completing his memoir, he died. But the general triumphed in his last battle. The memoir, which chronicles Grant's military career and ends with the close of the Civil War, sold like mad. More than three hundred thousand sets flew into eager hands, making it perhaps the bestseller of the century. Julia Grant received $450,000 in royalties (many millions in today's dollars). Historians consider Grant's work the finest military memoir in the English language. It has never gone out of print.

A passage of typical energy: "I at once put all the troops at Savannah in motion for Pittsburgh landing, knowing that the enemy was fortifying at Corinth and collecting an army there . . ."

Grant carried his relentless drive into all his wars, metaphorical as well as metaphysical. Let's take another look at the candor and conviction of his note to Dr. John H. Douglas. I think it's brilliant that he sees himself as a verb. It's a semantic idiosyncrasy, but why not? He was a man of action, after all. And if he saw himself as pure energy, that's undoubtedly more satisfying than puker of blood and prisoner of pain.

But what about Grant's definition of a verb, including *to suffer*? To answer this, let's take a little trip through time and dictionaries. My trusty *Webster's New World* dictionary, for instance, defines a verb as "any of a class of words expressing action, existence, or occurrence." Nothing about suffering.

However, I descend from a family that never throws out anything useful, and so I also possess a crumbling little dictionary from the 1850s. Smaller than a deck of cards, it's perfect for popping into a reticule. It's titled *Miniature Lexicon of the English Language*, edited by Lyman Cobb, a prolific textbook author and the chief competitor to Noah Webster. To give you a sense of this book's antiquated charms, in its pages the verb *conserve* means "to preserve or candy fruit."

It defines a verb as "one of the parts of speech, which signifies being, doing, or suffering."

Uncanny, no?

I'd like to think Grant knew this book. Did he have it beside him, as I have mine? Or was that simply the going definition in the Romantic era? In fact, the meaning of *suffer* has also changed through time. In general it has meant undergoing or experiencing something without succumbing, yet enduring pain and misery is not the only sense. At least as far back as the sixteenth century *suffer* included putting up with a person, as in the expression "to suffer fools gladly."

But an older definition—reaching back to the 1300s—suits our purpose here. From the *Oxford English Dictionary*: to suffer is "to be the object of an action, be acted upon, be passive." An example: "The Elements have power and force to do, whereas matter hath ability but only to suffer or to be wrought upon."

For that meaning, the *OED* also cites an example from the *Encyclopædia Metropolitana,* a British reference work from the mid-nineteenth century, which brings us back to Grant: It states that a verb "is a word which signifies to do, or to suffer, as well as to be."

"To suffer," in this sense, highlights the passive state of being acted upon by something. It's tempting to believe that Grant, in quoting the full definition of a verb, was pointing up this state of inactivity in himself. How poignant that in his last days, the career warrior embraced it all: assertive doing and resigned acceptance.

To be, to do, and to suffer—in the archaic sense—does sum up the impermanence and fluidity of human experience, doesn't it? We continually shift from doing and achieving things to having things acted upon us, even wrought upon us. To live is to change and suffer change, in ways both concrete and spiritual.

Therein lies a universe of possibilities. Grant, you could say, lived a great many of them. He was an indifferent West Point graduate who wanted nothing more than to teach math. He was a president who crushed the Ku Klux Klan during Reconstruction but in the end lost many of his gains. The war he'd won left enduring agonies through much of the nation, and at the end of his life, his own physical suffering was so extreme it was metaphoric.

Grant opens a vein in that introspective note to his doctor. He draws on his inner reservoir of feeling to locate a truth and offer an existential self-diagnosis. It's remarkable to see Grant express such an interior idea: I can't sleep, can't talk, and oh, by the way, I've left my body. I am the am, not the I.

I spoke about this note with fellow language enthusiast Mark Feeney, *The Boston Globe*'s Pulitzer-winning film and visual arts critic. Grant's pencil scrawl, he said, does what all great writing should do: "It changes how you see the world."

"This great man is dying, he knows he's dying, and instead of relaxing he's fighting his last campaign, writing this book so his family wouldn't starve. That he of all people should have this alertness to language is breathtaking," Feeney said. "Grant, who drank too much and had tobacco stains on his uniform. What an *idea* of himself. He didn't express himself in military terms; the point was verbal."

As Orwell insisted in "Politics and the English Language," clear thinking leads to clear writing and, pencil in hand, that is what Grant produced. His brief note—as well as his brisk, graceful memoir—unspooled from a writer who knew exactly what he wanted to say, and who chose clear, fresh images to say it.

In his memoir, his prose is direct, concise, muscular. It exhibits the same firm voice you hear in the doctor's note. It holds your attention, all swift running impulse and tight construction, with no confusion about its purpose.

At times, Grant's narration drops you into a dramatic scene: "The night was one of impenetrable darkness, with rain pouring down in torrents; nothing was visible to the eye except as revealed by the frequent flashes of lightning. Under these circumstances I had to trust the horse, without guidance, to keep the road."

He trusted himself, too, and believed his success lay in making quick decisions. On the fall of Fort Donelson, a major victory and turning point: "I saw the men standing in knots talking in the most excited manner. No officer seemed to be giving any directions." Grant heard the men's accounts of seeing Confederates carrying knapsacks full of rations, a sign they had fallen back from their charge and planned to retrench until provisions ran out. He knew that another Rebel force had started to steal away, and reasoning that the remaining line was vulnerable, Grant seized his chance.

"The one who attacks first now will be victorious. . . . I determined to make the assault at once on our left."

He grabbed the colonel and the two rushed on horseback to order an attack, telling the men as they passed to "fill your cartridge-boxes, quick, and get into line; the enemy is trying to escape and he must not be permitted to do so."

"This acted like a charm," he wrote. "The men only wanted some one to give them a command."

That taut, clear writing is the logical product of Grant's experience issuing high-stakes orders in battle. He never aspired to a literary or classic style, he noted in a letter; his writing "is just what it is pure and simple and nothing else."

As he composed his opus, Grant lost the ability to speak, but he never lost the gift of language and his intuitive sense of how best to use it. His memoir didn't address such private issues as his drinking problem, but neither did he lash out at critics, disrespect the enemy, or boast about his victories.

To take up Grant's idea and see him as a verb: What might it mean "to Ulysses Grant" a book, a battle, or a life? Certainly the definition could nod to specifics, such as staving off death by writing 360,000 vivid, coherent words in a single year and breaking publishing records.

But isn't it more significant, in contemplating the man and his words, to lift up the universals? "To Ulysses Grant" something: To set yourself to the task no matter the conditions and finish it. To write your story on your own terms and refuse to settle scores or gloat. To be, to do, to suffer, and, nevertheless, to persist.

* * *

Grant was not the first to describe himself figuratively as a verb. Henry Fielding, the English satirist, beat him to it with a spicy joke in his 1730 comedy play, *Rape upon Rape; or, The Justice Caught in His Own Trap.* A bold title, no doubt, and the play attacks immorality with bite. Take a look at this scene between the unscrupulous Justice Squeezum (one of theater's great names) and the more artful Hilaret, the lady who wants to trap him in the act. After coaxing coin from the lustful judge, Hilaret slyly asks what he expects her to do in return:

> **Squeezum:** You shall do—you shall do nothing. What I will do: I will be a Verb Active, and you shall be a Verb Passive.
>
> **Hilaret:** I wish you be not of the Neuter Gender.
>
> **Squeezum:** Why you little arch Rogue, do you understand *Latin*, hussy?

Squeezum, not just a lecher. A pretentious, *condescending* lecher.

But the exchange is priceless. (Little Arch Rogue: my secret self.)

In 1970, Buckminster Fuller, the polymathic architect-writer-inventor and creator of gleaming geodesic domes, published a concept book titled *I Seem to Be a Verb*. He collaborated with fellow experimentalist Jerome Agel and graphic designer Quentin Fiore, and the book is readable upside down as well as right side up. Among other musings, this fluid collection of art and essays proposes that nouns are confining while verbs are boundless.

"I live on Earth at present, and I don't know what I am. I know that I am not a category," Fuller wrote. "I am not a thing—a noun. I seem to be a verb, an evolutionary process—an integral function of the universe."

* * *

Let's pause on the idea of the verb as signifier of a metaphysical essence. This is the way Grant and Fuller applied it. "Verb" contained everything about them because they saw themselves as a process, whether driving it, as Fuller, or receiving it, as Grant. And they weren't wrong to use it in that way. The word *verb* started out as a very large idea, as we saw in chapter 2, the idea that verbs—all words asserting action or existence—are the most essential words of all.

Out of the mists of spirituality, etymology, and imagination, the verb floats before us meaning many things. I point this out not to confuse the subject—we are talking here, in this book, about writing, most of all—but as a reminder of the power of language and what a hold it has on our minds and visions.

Most of all, it seems to me, verbs tell us about change.

This leads me to what may seem a surprising turn: the Cherokee language, and its core ideas of connection and change.

Cherokee, or Tsalagi, written in the syllabary as ᏣᎳᎩ ᎦᏬᏂᎯᏍᏗ, is a verb-centric language in the extreme. Some sources estimate that it is *75 percent* verbs. (English, by comparison, is about 25 percent verbs.)

Cherokee verbs can undergo innumerable changes to mean different things and even tell whole stories in a single word, as we'll see. The tremendous power of these verbs stems from their inflections.

In grammar, inflections are the little changes added to a word to express different meanings. For example, in English, adding the inflection *-d* changes *bake* to *baked.* English verbs have but a handful of inflections, such as *-d, -ed,* or *-t* for past tenses, and the *-ing* forms. Any given Cherokee verb, though, may have *thousands* of possible inflections.

For this reason, a single verb can pack in so much information that it takes a whole sentence in English to translate it. I spoke about this with Benjamin Frey, a professor of Cherokee language and culture at the University of North Carolina Asheville.

"It's all about precision," he told me.

He brought up the word *widatsinegisi,* written as ᏫᏓᏥᏁᎩᏏ. It's built on the verb *pick up,* Frey said, but it contains various suffixes and prefixes that describe relationships. "There's 'Off in the distance' plus 'in the immediate future,'" he said, "plus 'I'm acting on a third person singular "it"' plus 'the object is a liquid' plus 'pick up.'

"People tell me, 'That's really complicated; when would you say such a thing?'" He chuckled. "Anytime you're going to get coffee."

The flexibility of Cherokee verbs "speaks to a language that keeps interrelatedness at the forefront of people's minds," Frey said. This is different from Indo-European languages, which include a sense of separation: "I'm a 'me,' and you must be a different entity from me."

For example, the meaning of *science,* in English, includes conducting experiments and dissecting something, taking it apart and studying its individual components. This clashes with the Cherokee philosophy of oneness with the wider natural world.

"How can you take apart anything in a world where everything is a closed system?" Frey said. "Everything's connected. So Cherokees need to know what English speakers really mean so they can translate it into their way of thinking." This might lead, he said, to creating a noun from the verbs for learning and ways of finding out.

When it comes to Cherokee verbs, the philosophy of interconnectedness is built in. *To teach* appears to be related to the verb *to circle*, to rotate around something, and Frey believes this springs from a holistic view of teaching as circling around a subject, to investigate every aspect of it and—just as important—its relationship to the rest of the world.

"If I'm going to teach you about a tree, we're going to walk around the tree so you can see the roots and the bark and the bugs walking on it, and you can see all the different perspectives," Frey said. The idea of circling mirrors his own experience as a child in Birmingham, Alabama, when his mother would take him to Oak Mountain State Park.

"She'd say, 'See this sassafras root? Smell it, hold it, touch it.' She'd stop me and say, 'Don't you hear the water? Listen.' She was teaching me all about the woods, and the network of relationships in the woods—you, the water, the roots, the birds."

Her teaching accepted the idea of not knowing everything, that it's crucial to see beyond the object (the noun) to the activity within and around it (the verbs). And to keep the senses open to such changes all around, Frey said.

"We need the earth and it needs us," he said. "We're the stewards of this place. That's how we understand our role as human beings."

The verbs spring from that philosophy, with their emphasis on relationships and associations and infinite change. This is a meaningful way to look at verbs, as describing more than action. They unfold new perspectives—and revelation. Perhaps this approaches the kind of thinking that prompted the dying Ulysses Grant, with his writer's imagination crackling like fire, and Buckminster Fuller, thrumming with optimism, to see themselves as verbs. As starbursts of new imaginings and as part of everything, all the profound and unknowable effects of the world.

Throughout this book I've set out the unique abilities of verbs to express meaning. Choose the right verb, precise and clear, and it speeds you along to saying what you mean. Assert your point with the active voice, use the passive voice with care and restraint. Opt for descriptive verbs and you can sweep away adverbs and other clutter. Moving beyond such essential pragmatics, we looked at the interpretive, poetic powers of verbs, how they can pull readers into your writing by suggesting and tantalizing, revealing the body's secrets, heightening emotion. In all these ways, verbs show change. From step to step—how high, how fast?—or point to point, and thought to thought. Whether changes of body, mind, or spirit, verbs put the process into words.

Nouns give us names, verbs show change. Grant was meditating on this in his final days, as he mused about his very existence as a verb and embodying everything a verb means. His body had passed from active to passive, yet his spirit still declared its evolving existence.

Change is not only an essential fact of life—it is, when you come down to it, what interests us most. What's going on? What's happening next door, across the street, back home? What discoveries and doings fill the news, what art is coming my way, what are *you* thinking about?

This is what I want you to take away. Verbs, boundless and new-forming, give you the means to grapple with this world of change and call it forth. Honor the verb, through everything you've learned in this book, and you possess the power to hold what vanishes. With verbs you can describe the innumerable separate tasks of life, yes, but also the circus. The flight, the wonder. You can imagine beyond your knowing and beyond your own transience. Verbs, in fact, bring you right up to the state of transience, because they delineate its existence. They are themselves transient and ephemeral but potent enough to seize an epiphany by the tail and show it off, if for a moment. They want only your choices, to measure the size of your imagination.

* * *

Good Habits

In past exercises, we've focused on using verbs to write about overt actions in physical spaces. This is an exercise in contemplation. Draw your attention inside; imagine the smallest action you can. Maybe it's your breath, your heartbeat, or your skin tingling from a slight chill in the air. Sit for a while. You might reflect on previous Good Habits: focusing on a subject and verb (chapter 1); zeroing in on the main idea (chapter 2); showing, not telling (chapter 4); expressing an emotion in verbs (chapter 6). Can you apply these techniques to writing about an interior sensation, such as the shape and texture of your thoughts? Or the flaring and passing of an emotion? Free-write for ten or fifteen minutes, jotting down every thought without stopping, even if it's "I don't feel anything, I don't feel anything." You will. Sit quietly and feelings may settle. Perhaps they'll rise and flutter away, or simmer, weigh, and press, or . . . ? List verbs that leap to mind: *breathe, remember, write, fritter, nudge* . . .

When you feel you've worked on this enough, scan your writing. What phrase, idea, or word can you build on? Start the process again, with that bit in mind; expand on it, refine it.

Writing about an inward state, like all writing, takes patience.

How does writing about inward action differ from writing about outward, visible action?

Here's another exercise in interior processes. Focus on your senses, one at a time (but not sight). Take a sip of water; how does it feel in your mouth? Sip again and write, tracing the water's path with verbs, describing the nuances in temperature and sensation. Smell an orange, a cup of tea, shampoo; conduct the same sensory experiment with words, focusing on verbs. Close your eyes and listen; write about the ambient sounds, how they strike your ear. Run your hand over the couch or your dog; curl it around a cup of coffee. What verbs describe the texture, the heat?

Afterword

> Writing can be described in two verbs: Throw up and clean up.
>
> —RAY BRADBURY

Creativity feeds on the stirring of your senses, on actions you see and do and glimpse beneath the surface. It feeds on all the flinging bits of life and how it feels when they strike you. "There is a vitality, a life force, an energy," said the great dance pioneer and choreographer Martha Graham, referring to her art. "A quickening that is translated through you into action."

How like writing. As you open yourself to your passions and enthusiasms, to your own life force, lock onto the power and subtleties of verbs to bring that deep essence into being. I hope this book inspires you to experiment in your writing. Play with the energy and expressiveness of verbs, and use them to awaken feelings in your readers.

Inspiring verbs are everywhere. Notice them and let them feed your imagination. In turn, *teach others to notice* through your writing. To notice how a workman slips out from the bushes like a cat, rests against a tree, and relishes a relaxing afternoon smoke. Or how a wild turkey emerges from the woods with her chicks, parading in the shadows like a fairy queen, then velvets into the undergrowth and disappears with her little ones scurrying behind.

Becoming a writer—improving as a writer—is an individual journey. It's not about memorizing writing techniques or following rules and formulas. Instead, wherever you find yourself on this road, commit to growth and change. Listen to yourself and others. Expand your scope to the world around you. Read with attention. Release truths from your mind however they come, in drips and drops, in torrents, in sloppy spills you mop up again and again until, underneath, you reveal something clean and bright. Beat on, against all currents; lose nothing to the unknown deeps.

I like this definition of writing, which a fellow author told me: mess, mess, mess, art.

Most of all, stay tuned to the drive inside.

Great writing comes from a mix of inspiration, personality, passion, and intelligence, and a manual won't supply it all. Only you will. The world needs your voice, and it awaits what you will create. Let these pages help it rise.

Here is Ernest Hemingway on his writing process:

> It was necessary to get exercise, to be tired in the body, and it was very good to make love with whom you loved. That was better than anything. But afterwards, when you were empty, it was necessary to read in order not to think or worry about your work until you could do it again.

Move, love, nourish the imagination. A self-propelling prescription for a creative, healthy, and pleasant life. And for good writing.

I wish you every bit of it.

✵ ✵ ✵

Good Habits

All writers know the gloom of getting stuck, of holding images in the mind that feel important and clear—while they flounder to find the words. Whether you call it writer's block or creative burnout, know that you can work through it. Here's one technique to try.

Imagine whatever you're working on as a scene in a movie. What is the atmosphere, the vibe? Is it tranquil, contemplative, frenetic, invigorating? Imagine the actions springing from that atmosphere—whether it's bodies at rest, flowers swaying on a slope, people mingling at a sherry party, or a Jeep bouncing along with a dog riding shotgun, spraying happy drool. Sink into this scene, feel its energy, envision the life within it. What verbs come to mind? Write vivid, descriptive, resonant verbs to fill in the main events, setting, and background of this scene. Compose plain, direct subject-verb sentences, filling in what has now become the start of your text.

ACKNOWLEDGMENTS

In researching this book I spoke to dozens of writers and editors about their craft. I owe immense thanks to Pat Myers, peerless maestro of the *Washington Post*'s Style copydesk, and Peter Kaufman, my sterling former editor at the *Post* and unrelated cousin-in-spirit. They read early drafts of the manuscript and opened my perspective, improved the book in innumerable ways, and saved me from just as many errors. (Those that remain are mine alone.) Poet and longtime officemate Tom Lachman provided the title and valuable insights. Jeffrey Seglin helped me see what this book could be and steered me to many key points and delicious examples. David E. Hoffman pointed me to important resources over encouraging kaffeeklatches. Many more writer friends and fellow journalists helped inspire and broaden my thoughts, including Henry Allen, John Archibald, Marc-Olivier Bherer, Austin Bogues, Kate Carlisle, James Castello, Beth Chang, Ellen Edwards, Robert Engelman, Mark Feeney, Sandra Fleishman, James Geary, Chris Jones, Vidya Krishnan, Naveen Kumar, Peter Lattman, Christine Ledbetter, Vince Rinehart, and Allen Sviridoff.

I'm profoundly grateful for the attentions of Casey Denis, my perceptive editor at Penguin Press, and for the careful copyediting and stewardship of the entire Penguin team, including Sarah Hutson, Victoria Laboz, Daniel Lagin, Lauren Lauzon, Randee Marullo, Mollie Reid, and Susan VanHecke. Ben Wiseman designed the knockout cover—wow, and thanks. At Penguin Press UK, I had the good fortune of working with Chloe Currens, Eleanor Cousins Brown, Louis Cluzan, and Julie Woon. Thank you all for your spectacular care, expertise, and creativity. My agent, Barney Karpfinger, is an inexhaustible reservoir of ideas and his enthusiasm shone over this whole process. To Barney, and to Sam Chidley: gratitude overflowing.

I leaned on the Buncombe County Public Libraries and owe particular thanks to the North Asheville librarians.

There's no better laboratory for testing ideas than the classroom. I'm grateful to all my students across the years for what they've taught me and for helping me refine my views on writing and teaching.

My gratitude extends to the encouragement and good humor of my family, especially my mother, who from earliest memory fueled my inquiries into words and led me on life-shaping adventures in books, art, and theater. My stepmother, a wise, gentle friend, fed my curiosity about science and the natural world. Neither of these extraordinary women lived to see this book in final form but their lives continue to inspire me. I'm grateful for the patience and understanding of my book-loving father, who looked the other way when I blew off bedtime, reading by penlight; and for Zeke, Asa, Annabel, Phounam, and Genevieve, who keep me wondering how I ever got so lucky and who suffered with me when *Baggage* reruns disappeared.

This book wouldn't exist without the steadying care of my husband, John, who always knew when the day required riverside tacos (before Hurricane Helene's rampage), and when to buckle up for another exciting tangent on, oh, the exact ordering of all the different types of adjectives. What I've written here, not to mention everything else, is better for his thinking.

Finally, I'm grateful to Zelda Fitzgerald. Halfway through writing this book, we moved into a house that, according to legend, was home to Scott's wife and muse, a dedicated dancer and artist in her own right. She spent her final years in Asheville, and the story goes that at some point, Zelda stayed in the room that is my office. The coincidence feels significant; her husband's work weaves through my reading life as well as through these pages. Whether the story is true or not, it's a reminder that none of us creates alone. I thank Zelda for her inspiration and for being the best ghost a ballet-loving *Gatsby* fangirl could ever have.

APPENDIX

The verb treasury of the English language is rich with beautiful verbs to rediscover. Here are some vintage verbs in usable condition and worth reviving, from our language attic:

Batten: to strengthen or fasten. We know this for the nautical cry "Batten down the hatches!" But there's so much else we can batten—storm windows, resolve.

Braze: to solder with brass.

Cere: to cover with wax.

Concatenate: to link together or join, as in a chain or series.

For example: When we reached the summit, we saw spots of mist concatenating in the valley below, winding through it like a snake.

Conglobate: to gather together into a round mass.

Endue: to supply with mental excellences.

In *Charlotte's Web*, for instance, E. B. White endues a spider with great skills in writing and friendship.

My little Lyman Cobb lexicon from the 1850s makes clear that there's a subtle difference between *endue* and *endow*, which suggests a more material quality. *Endue* springs from the Anglo-French *enduire* and Latin *inducere*, both meaning "to lead." Its first known use was in the fifteenth century.

Hurkle: By itself, *hurkle* means to sit huddled in a crouched position either for warmth or secrecy. Adding *durkle* gives it a dose of whimsy, and you get a harmless, joyous revolt that's fun to say (and do).

Hurkle-durkle: to lounge in bed long after it's time to get up. (See the story about this in chapter 9.)

Intenerate: This verb, dating back to 1576 and meaning "to make tender" or "to soften," seems especially right for poetry.

Prolect: to form in the mind.

Rantipole: to act in a wild, unruly manner.

He rantipoles through life like a rocker settling scores at the Hotel du Cap.

Don't you wish you could rantipole, just once, with good insurance? *Rantipole* smells like rough leather and beer; it dusts the air when you shake it. It's lived a hard, well-traveled, raucous life. A jewel of an archaic verb, indeed. But *rantipole*'s etymology is guesswork. Fitting, no? Probably from *ranty* + *pole*, meaning "head" (alteration of *poll*). It dates at least to the eighteenth century, when rantipoling rantipoles undoubtedly had tremendous if less expensive fun.

Raven: to devour greedily.

Hopped up on vitamins, Snowball burst through the cat door and began ravening all the little birds.

This version of *raven* is no avian creature. From the fifteenth-century Middle French *raviner*, to seize or pillage, and Latin *rapina*, an act of plunder or pillage (also sources of the adjective *ravenous*). Among our verbs of violence, *raven* carries the sense of a predator's weaponry against hunger—and its prey.

Recrudesce: to break out again.

As COVID cases recrudesce, take care of yourself and those around you.

A fabulous, lost verb, with so many possibilities. Thank you, eighteenth century. From the Latin *recrudescere*, to become raw again—who knew there was a complete word for that?—*re* + *crudescere*, and from *crudus*, raw (where we get *crude* and *cruel* as well). In medical and historical contexts you may see the noun *recrudescence*, meaning a new outbreak after a period of inactivity. May the original source—the verb form with a lively, dramatic rhythm—recrudesce.

Stupe: to foment.

Tossicate: to upset, agitate, or disturb. But I bet you can guess that from the sound of it, which makes it fun. A great word to hiss in an undertone: Don't tossicate your dad, hon, or he'll hide the keys to the car.

NOTES

xvi **"So we beat on":** This and all subsequent passages from F. Scott Fitzgerald, *The Great Gatsby* (Charles Scribner's Sons, 1925).

CHAPTER 1: ENERGIZE

5 **"Eva Perón tears the shoes":** Sarah L. Kaufman, "A New Ballet Tips 'Evita' Perón off Her Pedestal," *Washington Post*, December 1, 2022, https://www.washingtonpost.com/theater-dance/2022/12/01/dona-peron-evita-ballet-hispanico/.

5 **classic rule of journalism:** See Primo Levi, *The Periodic Table*, trans. Raymond Rosenthal (Penguin, 2012).

6 **"As soon as I realized":** Sally Rooney, *Beautiful World, Where Are You* (Farrar, Straus and Giroux, 2021).

7 **verb for a jumping motion:** I'm indebted to Dan I. Slobin at the University of California, Berkeley, for these examples and more on manner-of-motion verbs in his interesting chapter "What Makes Manner of Motion Salient? Explorations in Linguistic Typology, Discourse, and Cognition," in *Space in Languages: Linguistic Systems and Cognitive Categories*, ed. M. Hickmann and S. Robert (John Benjamins, 2006), 59–81.

8 **"All they do is chatter":** John Logan, *Red* (Oberon Books Ltd, 2009), scene 5, 65.

8 **"Alice came to":** Rooney, *Beautiful World, Where Are You*, 39.

13 **"WAITING FOR THE 8TH":** Eli Saslow, "Waiting for the 8th," *Washington Post*, December 15, 2013, washingtonpost.com/sf/national/2013/12/15/waiting-for-the-8th.

17 **"'Do you remember the lake?'":** Virginia Woolf, *Mrs Dalloway* (Harcourt, Brace & World, 1925), 64.

CHAPTER 2: CURATE

21 **"But if these massive forms":** Roberta Smith, "Richard Serra, Who Recast Sculpture on a Massive Scale, Dies at 85," *New York Times*, March 26, 2024, nytimes.com/2024/03/26/arts/richard-serra-dead.html.

25 **"But now, though":** Sigrid Nunez, *The Friend* (Riverhead, 2018), 134.

26 **These verb synergies:** This is what Finn Wolfhard of *Stranger Things* fame did when Jimmy Fallon ribbed him with "Can you read?" Quick-witted Finn fired back, "Can you host?," https://www.youtube.com/watch?v=iMM067PI1oM.

28 **"A few days later":** Sujatha Gidla, *Ants Among Elephants: An Untouchable Family and the Making of Modern India* (Farrar, Straus & Giroux, 2017), 195.

30 **"He waited the coming":** Flannery O'Connor, *The Complete Stories* (Farrar, Straus & Giroux, 1971), 382.

32 **"Through the day":** Willa Cather, *O Pioneers!* (Signet Classics, 1989), 17.

32 **"The body dies":** Wallace Stevens, *Poems by Wallace Stevens* (Vintage, 1959), 5–6.

33 **"In the brick houses":** John Dos Passos, *Manhattan Transfer* (Harper & Brothers, 1925).

35 **"White-stone-cobbled streets":** Hisham Matar, *In the Country of Men* (Dial, 2006), 26–27.

37 **His expectation was to set sail:** Some possibilities: 1. **He planned** to leave as soon as he got the inheritance check from his parents. 2. To meet the new delivery requirement, the **main office needs** to expand the workforce (or increase hiring). 3. Any incoming **leader faces** the challenge of managing campaign staff.

CHAPTER 3: TAKE A STAND

42 **"News about the 1918":** I adapted my examples from material in this excellent article by Becky Little, "As the 1918 Flu Emerged, Cover-Up and Denial Helped It Spread," history.com, last updated May 28, 2025, history.com/news/1918-pandemic-spanish-flu-censorship.

43 **Nixon's press secretary:** James Fallows, "'Mistakes Were Made,'" *The Atlantic*, February 19, 2015, theatlantic.com/politics/archive/2015/02/mistakes-were-made/385663.

44 **"Deportations *were launched*":** Kathleen J. Fitzgerald, "A Sociology of Race/Ethnicity Textbooks: Avoiding White Privilege, Ahistoricism, and Use of the Passive Voice," *Sociological Focus*, 45, no. 4 (2012): 338–57, http://www.jstor.org/stable/41633924.

44 **"a weapon of discourse":** David Barsamian, "Interview with John Pliger, *Progressive Magazine*, July 16, 2007, progressive.org/magazine/interview-john-pliger.

46 **Orwell rages against:** George Orwell, *A Collection of Essays* (Harcourt Brace Jovanovich, 1953).

50 **"During the meeting ":** John Appleby, "Letter: This Is No Way to Build a City," *Mountain Xpress*, August 17, 2024, mountainx.com/opinion/letter-this-is-no-way-to-build-a-city.

53 **". . . feet padded into":** Toni Morrison, *The Bluest Eye* (Vintage, 2007), 12.

54 **"originated in envy":** Morrison, *The Bluest Eye*, 122.

55 **"George Floyd, the Minnesota man":** Erin Donaghue, "Two Autopsies Both Find George Floyd Died by Homicide, but Differ on Some Key Details," CBS

News, June 4, 2020, https://www.cbsnews.com/news/george-floyd-death-autopsies-homicide-axphyxiation-details/.

57 **"Large and consistent decreases":** "Climate Change Indicators: Snowpack," US Environmental Protection Agency, last updated May 9, 2025, epa.gov/climate-indicators/climate-change-indicators-snowpack.

57 **"Although most of the valley's":** William A. Matthews III, *The Geologic Story of Palo Duro Canyon, Guidebook 8* (Bureau of Economic Geology/University of Texas at Austin, 1983).

57 **"In 1933 the recreational":** Matthews, *The Geologic Story of Palo Duro Canyon.*

59 **"Stately, plump Buck Mulligan":** James Joyce, *Ulysses* (Vintage Classics Edition, 1990), 3.

59 **"In town he drank":** Sherwood Anderson, *The Triumph of the Egg* (Four Walls Eight Windows, 1921), 46.

60 **"Usually this omelette":** Juliet Corson, *A Course of Lectures on the Principles of Domestic Economy and Cookery* (Pioneer Press Company, 1887), 15, https://www.gutenberg.org/cache/epub/35567/pg35567-images.html.

CHAPTER 4: SHARPEN

63 **"In fact, she realized":** From Julie Anne Long, *The Beast Takes a Bride* (Avon, 2024).

70 **"The pianist races along":** From Sarah L. Kaufman, "Choreographer Justin Peck's Unprecedented Success with New York City Ballet," *Washington Post*, March 29, 2014, https://www.washingtonpost.com/entertainment/theater_dance/choreographer-justin-pecks-unprecedented-success-with-new-york-city-ballet/2014/03/27/9a6873dc-b43b-11e3-8cb6-284052554d74_story.html.

78 **"When the barber threw back":** John Dos Passos, *Manhattan Transfer* (Harper & Brothers, 1925), section 2, "Metropolis."

78 **"A troop of young soldiers":** Zadie Smith, *Swing Time* (Penguin Press, 2016), 267.

79 **"Emma returned to him":** Gustave Flaubert, *Madame Bovary* (Norton, 2005), 222.

80 **"an admirable painting":** Flaubert, *Madame Bovary*, 328.

80 **"Less than two weeks":** Dick Andros, "Fanny Elssler (1810–1884)," Andros on Ballet, April 1993, michaelminn.net/andros/biographies/elssler_fanny.

CHAPTER 5: WEED

88 **"'You've let the spurious'":** Both examples from Sabrina Jeffries, *Never Seduce a Scoundrel* (Pocket Books, 2006).

90 **"'This is a really good business'":** Elahe Izadi and Will Sommer, "*Washington Post* Cuts Follow Rapid Expansion, Unmet Revenue Projections," October 11, 2023, washingtonpost.com/style/media/2023/10/11/washington-post-buyouts-metro-cuts.

90 **told *Fortune* magazine:** Charlotte Hampton and Bloomberg, "Fearing Social Media Backlash, Companies Are Using All Kinds of Euphemisms to Avoid Being Straightforward About Layoffs. 'Jargon monoxide,'" *Fortune*, February 10, 2024, https://fortune.com/2024/02/10/layoffs-euphemisms-ceo-social-media-backlash/.

91 **“Hear the links”:** Elizabeth Jennings, *New Collected Poems* (Carcanet, 2002), 223.

CHAPTER 6: TANTALIZE

96 **“do you love him Caddy”:** William Faulkner, *The Sound and the Fury* (Vintage, 1954), 203.

98 **“Chester’s heart stumbled”:** Patricia Highsmith, *The Two Faces of January* (Atlantic Monthly Press, 1988), 25.

99 **“To pack the Bud”:** From *The Complete Poems of Emily Dickinson*, ed. Thomas H. Johnson (Little, Brown and Company, 1961).

102 **“Mr Grant did as he was told”:** Angela Thirkell, *The Brandons* (Alfred A. Knopf, 1939), 200.

103 **“I went back”:** Tim O’Brien, *The Things They Carried* (Mariner Books, 2009).

CHAPTER 7: NOTICE

108 **“The unpracticed novelist”:** James Wood, *How Fiction Works* (Picador, 2008), 96.

109 **“If you can find a way”:** Sarah L. Kaufman, “Rita Moreno on Strength, Stamina and the Power of a Killer Body,” *Washington Post,* July 10, 2014, washingtonpost.com/entertainment/theater_dance/rita-moreno-on-strength-stamina-and-the-power-of-a-killer-body/2014/07/10/5882a6a6-0858-11e4-8a6a-19355c7e870a_story.html.

109 **“The set of his shoulders”:** George Orwell, *Down and Out in Paris and London* (Harcourt, 1933), 68–69.

111 **“Pitch after pitch”:** Sarah L. Kaufman, “The Art of the World Series,” *Sarah Kaufman,* October 27, 2019, sarahlkaufman.com/blog.

111 **“Clark dribbled strongly”:** Sally Jenkins, “Caitlin Clark Is Shining—and Making Her Skeptics Look Silly,” *Washington Post,* August 27, 2024, washingtonpost.com/sports/2024/08/27/caitlin-clark-is-shining-making-her-skeptics-look-silly.

112 **“Cobb despised the medical”:** Al Stump’s “The Fight to Live” appeared in *True* magazine in 1961, and is anthologized in *The Art of Fact: A Historical Anthology of Literary Journalism,* ed. by Kevin Kerrane and Ben Yagoda (Touchstone, 1997), 273.

113 **“I contributed to a lot”:** Thomas Germain, “AI Took Their Jobs. Now They Get Paid to Make It Sound Human,” BBC, June 16, 2024, bbc.com/future/article/20240612-the-people-making-ai-sound-more-human.

116 **“The garden was long”:** Zadie Smith, *Swing Time* (Penguin Press, 2016), 21.

CHAPTER 8: ZHUZH IT UP

119 **burst of insight:** For more on the power of metaphor, see James Geary’s wonderful, definitive book *I Is an Other: The Secret Life of Metaphor and How It Shapes the Way We See the World* (HarperCollins, 2011).

121 **“The first streetcar”:** James Thurber, *My Life and Hard Times* (Harper & Brothers, 1933), 26.

122 **“It was not enough”:** Robert Benchley, “The Last of the Heath Hens,” *New Yorker,* May 6, 1933, newyorker.com/magazine/1933/05/06/the-last-of-the-heath-hens.

124 **"Falsehood flies, and Truth":** Jonathan Swift, "The Art of Political Lying," in *The Examiner*, no. 14, November 9, 1710, https://archive.org/details/jonathan-swift-the-examiner-14-the-art-of-political-lying-november-9-1710/page/9/mode/2up?q=limping. Also quoted in *The Yale Book of Quotations*, ed. Fred R. Shapiro (Yale University Press, 2006), 615.

124 **"She could feel the countless":** Edith Wharton, *The House of Mirth* (Library of America, 1905), 338.

124 **"Her welter of apologies":** Jennifer Egan, *A Visit from the Goon Squad* (Alfred A. Knopf, 2010), 126.

126 **"The sand-hills here run down":** Wilkie Collins, *The Moonstone* (Penguin Classics, 1998), 36.

127 **"On the second rise":** E. M. Forster, *A Passage to India* (Harcourt, 1984), 4–5.

129 **"We never enjoyed a pipe":** J. E. Taylor et al., *Collecting and Preserving: Notes on Collecting and Preserving Natural-History Objects* (London: W. H. Allen, 1883).

130 **"But now the Clouds":** Thomas Parnell, "The Hermit," in *Poems on Several Occasions: Written by Dr. Thomas Parnell, Late Arch-Deacon of Clogher: and Published by Mr. Pope* (London: B. Lintot, 1722 [1721]), 164–80, eighteenthcenturypoetry.org/works/o4106-w0190.shtml.

CHAPTER 9: CIGARETTE ME

137 **creating verbs from nouns:** Eve V. Clark and Herbert H. Clark, "When Nouns Surface as Verbs," *Language* 55, no. 4 (December 1979): 767–811.

138 **"In fact, for a political":** Will Welch, "The Memeing of Life," *GQ*, September 2024.

139 **"Despite the loud":** Sarah L. Kaufman, "Merce Cunningham's Choice Chances," *Washington Post*, October 16, 2003.

140 **"*rawdogging* ended up":** "2024 Word of the Year Is 'Rawdog,'" American Dialect Society, January 10, 2025, americandialect.org/2024-word-of-the-year-is-rawdog.

140 **"Here is how platforms die":** "2023 Word of the Year Is 'Enshittification,'" American Dialect Society, January 5, 2024, americandialect.org/2023-word-of-the-year-is-enshittification.

142 **"You will likely be rewarded":** Chris Yount, "Naming Your Brand: Control the Verb, Control the Market," *Forbes*, July 28, 2020, forbes.com/councils/forbesbusinessdevelopmentcouncil/2020/07/28/naming-your-brand-control-the-verb-control-the-market.

143 **"I ♥ a Hate-Watch":** Alissa Wilkinson, "I ♥ a Hate-Watch. Don't You?," *New York Times*, August 19, 2021, nytimes.com/2024/08/19/arts/television/hate watching-emily-in-paris.html.

147 **"He stood alone":** Ocean Vuong, *Time Is a Mother* (Penguin Press, 2022).

147 **"blackberrying in the sun":** Virginia Woolf, *Mrs Dalloway* (Harcourt, Brace & World, 1925), 70.

CHAPTER 10: STIMULATE

150 **when they hit each other:** Ann Marsh and Greta Lorge, "How the Truth Gets Twisted," *Stanford Magazine*, November/December 2012, stanfordmag.org/contents/how-the-truth-gets-twisted.

152 **"Why would they not":** Edgar Allan Poe, *The Works of Edgar Allan Poe,* vol. 2, *The Raven Edition* (n.p., n.d.), gutenberg.org/files/25525/old/25525-h/files/2148-h/2148-h.htm#link2H_4_0019.

153 **mind is a full-body:** Anežka Kuzmičová, "Literary Narrative and Mental Imagery: A View from Embodied Cognition," *Style* 48, no. 3 (Fall 2014): 275–93, jstor.org/stable/10.5325/style.48.3.275.

154 **"as if he were ambling":** Sarah L. Kaufman, "Behind the Scenes at Verizon Center: Building the Set for J-Lo and Iglesias," *Washington Post,* August 1, 2012, washingtonpost.com/lifestyle/style/behind-the-scenes-at-verizon-center-building-a-set-with-136000-pounds-of-equipment/2012/08/01/gJQAYkAtPX_story.html.

154 **"The pleasure of the text":** Roland Barthes, *The Pleasure of the Text,* trans. Richard Miller (Hill and Wang, 1975).

156 **our "motor program":** George Lakoff and Mark Johnson, *Philosophy in the Flesh: The Embodied Mind and Its Challenge to Western Thought* (Basic Books, 1999).

157 **brains show activity:** Benjamin K. Bergen, phone interview with author, October 2023.

159 **they use nouns and prepositions:** For more on this, see, for example, Jean M. Mandler's chapter, "How to Talk About Motion Without Verbs," in *Dynamism in Metaphor and Beyond,* ed. Herbert L. Colston, Teenie Matlock, and Gerard J. Steen (John Benjamins, 2022), 293.

160 **in activity-oriented speech:** Soonja Choi and Alison Gopnik, "Early Acquisition of Verbs in Korean: A Cross-Linguistic Study," *Journal of Child Language* 22, no. 3 (1995): 497–529.

161 **phenomenon of simulation:** See, for example, Greg J. Stephens, Lauren J. Silbert, and Uri Hasson, "Speaker–Listener Neural Coupling Underlies Successful Communication," *Proceedings of the National Academy of Sciences* 107, no. 32 (2010): 14425–30, pnas.org/doi/10.1073/pnas.1008662107; and Mikkel Wallentin et al., "Amygdala and Heart Rate Variability Responses from Listening to Emotionally Intense Parts of a Story," *NeuroImage* 58, no. 3 (October 2011): 963–73, sciencedirect.com/science/article/abs/pii/S1053811911007233; and these resources: Lisa Cron, *Wired for Story* (Ten Speed Press, 2012); and "The Storytelling Animal: Jonathan Gottschall at TEDxFurmanU," TEDx Talks, May 4, 2014, youtube.com/watch?v=Vhd0XdedLpY.

162 **"He was invaded":** James Baldwin, *Go Tell It on the Mountain* (Vintage, 2024).

163 **"It changed everything":** Alan Hollinghurst, *Our Evenings* (Random House, 2024), 396.

164 **using monster metaphors:** Teenie Matlock, Chelsea Coe, and A. Leroy Westerling, "Monster Wildfires and Metaphor in Risk Communication," *Metaphor and Symbol* 32, no. 4 (2017): 250–61, doi.org/10.1080/10926488.2017.1384273.

165 **"The sky in northern Alberta's":** Holly Yan, David Williams, and Chuck Johnston, "Fort McMurray Fire: Entire City Forced to Flee as Inferno Rages," CNN, May 4, 2016, cnn.com/2016/05/04/world/fort-mcmurray-fire-canada/index.html.

165 **"Entire neighborhoods burned":** John Vaillant, *Fire Weather* (Alfred A. Knopf, 2023), 4.

167 **"John *was painting*":** Teenie Matlock et al., "Smashing New Results on Aspectual Framing: How People Talk About Car Accidents," *Studies in Language* 36, no. 3 (2012): 699–720, doi.org/10.1075/sl.36.3.09mat.

CHAPTER 11: TRANSFORM

171 **"I do not sleep":** Note dated July 1885 in *Ulysses S. Grant: Memoirs and Selected Letters*, ed. Mary McFeely and William S. McFeely (Library of America, 1990), 1120.

172 **gruesome terminal disease:** Ron Chernow, *Grant* (Penguin Books, 2018), 931.

172 **finest military memoir:** "The Personal Memoirs of Ulysses S. Grant: The Complete Annotated Edition," Ulysses S. Grant Presidential Library, accessed August 31, 2024, usgrantlibrary.org/node/54.

172 **"I at once put all the troops":** Ulysses S. Grant, *Personal Memoirs of U. S. Grant*, ed. Mary McFeely and William S. McFeely (Library of America, 1990), 222.

173 **"to suffer fools gladly":** "For ye suffre foles gladly because that ye youreselves are wyse," 2 Corinthians 6 (Tyndale, 1526).

173 **"to be the object":** *Oxford English Dictionary*, "suffer (*v.*), sense I.4," September 2024, doi.org/10.1093/OED/9232736902.

173 **"The Elements have power":** "The Elements haue power and force to do, whereas matter hath abilitie but onely to suffer or to be wrought vppon," Philippe De Mornay, *A Woorke Concerning the Trewnesse of the Christian Religion*, trans. Philip Sidney and Arthur Golding (London: Thomas Cadman, 1587).

173 **"is a word which signifies":** John Stoddart, "Grammar," in *Encyclopædia metropolitana: or, Universal dictionary of knowledge*, ed. Edward Smedley, vol. 1 (London: B. Fellowes et al., 1845).

175 **"The night was one of":** Grant, *Personal Memoirs of U. S. Grant*, 205.

175 **"is just what it is":** Chernow, *Grant*, 944.

176 **"You shall do":** Henry Fielding, *Rape upon Rape; or, The Justice Caught in His Own Trap* (London: J. Wats, 1730), act 2, scene 5, archive.org/details/bim_eighteenth-century_rape-upon-rape-or-the-_fielding-henry_1730/page/n29/mode/2up?view=theater.

177 **"I live on Earth":** R. Buckminster Fuller with Jerome Agel and Quentin Fiore, *I Seem to Be a Verb* (Bantam Books, 1970), epigraph, https://archive.org/details/i-seem-to-be-a-verb-buckminster-fuller/page/n1/mode/2up?q=%22I+live+on+Earth+at+present%22&view=theater.

AFTERWORD

183 **"There is a vitality":** Agnes De Mille, *Martha: The Life and Work of Martha Graham* (Random House, 1991), 264.

184 **"It was necessary":** Ernest Hemingway, *A Moveable Feast* (Charles Scribner's Sons, 1964), 25–26.

FURTHER RESOURCES

Bradbury, Ray. *Zen in the Art of Writing: Releasing the Creative Genius Within You.* Bantam, 1992.

Brohaugh, William. *Write Tight: How to Keep Your Prose Sharp, Focused and Concise.* Writer's Digest Books, 1993.

Caldarone, Marina, and Maggie Lloyd-Williams. *Actions: The Actors' Thesaurus.* Drama Publishers, 2004.

Clark, Roy Peter. *Writing Tools: 55 Essential Strategies for Every Writer.* Little, Brown, 2006.

Day, Robert A., and Nancy Sakaduski. *Scientific English: A Guide for Scientists and Other Professionals.* Greenwood, 2011.

Dreyer, Benjamin. *Dreyer's English: An Utterly Correct Guide to Clarity and Style.* Random House, 2019.

Ferrante, Elena. *In the Margins: On the Pleasures of Reading and Writing.* Translated by Ann Goldstein. Europa Editions, 2022.

Geary, James. *I Is an Other: The Secret Life of Metaphor and How It Shapes the Way We See the World.* HarperCollins, 2011.

Lamott, Anne. *Bird by Bird: Some Instructions on Writing and Life.* Anchor Books, 1995.

Maugham, W. Somerset. *The Summing Up.* Pocket Books, 1967.

Petras, Ross, and Kathryn Ross. *That Doesn't Mean What You Think It Means: The 150 Most Commonly Misused Words and Their Tangled Histories.* Ten Speed Press, 2018.

Pinker, Steven. *The Sense of Style: The Thinking Person's Guide to Writing in the 21st Century.* Penguin, 2015.

Plotnik, Arthur. *Spunk & Bite: A Writer's Guide to Bold, Contemporary Style.* Diversified Publishing, 2007.

Wood, James. *How Fiction Works.* Picador, 2008.

Zinsser, William. *On Writing Well: An Informal Guide to Writing Nonfiction.* HarperPerennial, 1990.